MEADOW

MEADOW

NICHOLAS POLLACK

HIRMER

for my parents

The photographs in this book are made in and along the edges of what is, by several measures, one of the world's most formidable salt marshes, a wildly under-appreciated place where fresh water from faraway rivers mixes with salt water from the sea. The water in this marsh is brackish and tidal, currents shifting throughout the day and the seasons—though to be sure, the water is complicated by what comes off the shores all around it. Pollutants and toxins seep from the great hills of trash that make up the panorama of this place, and then there is the long list of contaminants that run off the roads that crisscross this giant wetland, that are injected as sewage by the communities living on its shores or in the hills far upstream. And yet like salt marshes everywhere, this one's once-industrialized edges are cleansed each day by the tides, a daily baptism, repeated for millennia, only now, the tides, while not getting tired, are changing: in just the past half century, or since around World War II, the seas themselves have become increasingly tainted. Oceans, once thought of as infinite, are today infected with the finality of plastics, by waves made acidic, by the carbon we insist on pumping into the air that oceans, like us, breathe to stay alive.

The particular body of water along which these photos are made is called Penhorn Creek. It is one of many tidal creeks flowing in and out of what is variously referred to as the Secaucus Meadows, the Jersey Meadows, the Meadows or simply the Meadowlands. Whereas once the meadows were called meadows because of vast green fields of spartina grass, known in the nineteenth century as salt hay, today they are meadows due largely to the presence of the most common reed in the world—phragmites, though note that spartina is still there and has been and continues to be planted, part of the marsh's most recent comeback. But despite the resurgence of grasses, and despite the enduring vitality of ecological functions in a place that, while tested, never went away, the Meadowlands are still, in too many quarters, reviled or just ignored or rushed past. At the very least they are dismally underrecognized as the ecological centerpiece of the region and mistaken either for the end of the world or as an in-between, a segue between Newark and Jersey City, or depending on how precise your map settings are, between New York City and the rest of the world. It's a wasteland that's out of sight, depending on who is doing the looking, depending on what it is they see.

And the place is devastated, it's true. Toxins in soils. Streams robbed of oxygen, impounded variously by the New Jersey Turnpike in the 1950s or by a plan to develop the area as a dairy farm in the late 1800s. It's hard to imagine a place more beat-up, or, frankly, shit on, though, sadly, it's not that hard. Love Canal jumps to mind, and the 21,000 tons of toxic industrial waste that had to be excavated from that Niagara Falls neighborhood, leading to the formation of the federal Superfund program in 1980. Today the Environmental Protection Agency lists close to 1,400 Superfund sites, in fact, scattered around North America, and the Meadowlands hosts maybe more than its share. But what if we have the Meadowlands and its devastation backwards? What if we consider the devastation not for what's devastated but for what has survived? What if we turn ourselves around to see the giant estuary bisected by I-95 as a centerpiece instead of an edge, as a place to start to think again about how we live?

*

I'll admit that that when I first visited the Meadowlands, as a kid at the end of the 1970s, I thought the place was the end of the world. I attribute this in part to my first trip being accidental. I meant to drive across the Meadowlands, on a highway, but accidentally drove right about where (coincidentally) you can look across to Penhorn Creek. I was in high school at the time, and I'd borrowed my parents' car, to drive to a performance by the band Yes, at Madison Square Garden, my friends navigating, or trying to. Coming from New Jersey, we took a wrong turn, and instead flying across the great arch of concrete that is the New Jersey

Turnpike, or rattling up and over the then-rusting Erector Set bridge that is the Pulaski Skyway, we wound up being lost underneath the Skyway, in Kearny, New Jersey, just briefly, though long enough to be spooked by a distinctly Sopranos vibe, roughly two decades prior to the airing of *The Sopranos*.

I remember we made it back onto the highway, and to do so we had to drive through a wall of steam. It was terrifying; little blue signs for the Holland Tunnel, seemingly randomly posted, were like faint rescue beacons. After that first trip, I returned to the Meadowlands on purpose, over and over, in my twenties and then my thirties, and after I moved west for a decade, I returned with a different idea about the place. The Jersey Meadows, I had realized, aren't the edges of the New York-New Jersey metropolitan area. Penhorn Creek isn't at the periphery. The Meadowlands are a center, the geographic heart of the giant estuary that powers the waters around New York and New Jersey, reaching south and east into the Raritan River system, that connects the Meadowlands north and east into the Long Island Sound and up into Canada and all of the Atlantic.

And it's hard to oversell the power of the estuary just as it is hard to oversell the power of our actions toward it. In my lifetime—born in the 60s, voting by 1981, aware of the climate warming by about 1989—the U.S. officially changed its mind on water and wetlands. Prior to 1972, you could dump what you wanted into streams and rivers. You could inject sewage into salt marshes, and you could dump industrial effluents into the wetlands that feed the streams and protect riverside human settlements from flooding. (Plenty of people knew that these were all bad ideas, but government only does what it's asked.) Then came the Clean Water Act, which changed the game: suddenly, polluting water was against the law and wetlands were protected. The law's intent has suffered from dilution over the years, thanks to developers and their lawyers and a never-ending sense that business knows what's best for the nation, even when capitalism has no problem devaluing and devouring people in addition to all the rest of the living world. But generally speaking, fresh water in America has transformed in my lifetime from being occasionally flammable and sometimes pudding-like dreck, to a clear, clean fluid that is swimmable in New York Harbor on a good day.

And in the forty years since I saw Yes at the Garden, the Meadowlands has gone from being staked out by the FBI as a possible dumping site for the Mob (at the PCP Landfill, south of Penhorn Creek on the Hackensack, a site that is now a park) to being littered with parks and canoe launches. Groups like the Hackensack River Keeper have worked tirelessly to help the estuary reestablish its natural ecological functions—replanting spartina marshes, planting oyster habitat, and cleaning up local streams, for instance—while pushing to set aside more land, to spare a Great Plains-like vista that has been in some ways left alone for the last half a century, after massive industry pulled out. Are there plenty of setbacks? Yes, among them the construction of a retail and entertainment complex named (of all things) American Dream, the biggest mall in the world for the moment and, in terms of parking lots and imperviousness, a nightmare. Also problematic are some of the plans that have come into the region from outside, seeing the communities that reside along the meadows as stakeholders (a planning and development term) rather than as human.

*

I have a theory about saving the world. I call it the plastic chair theory. It goes like this: a plastic chair set down beside a river or a stream or a marsh—and specifically a chair set up in a place that is devoid of parks and manicured waterfronts—is a marker. It marks a portal or a gateway, a place where a body (in this case a live body, setting aside the notion of mob burials) has sat and maybe fished or drank a beer or a coffee and in the meantime looked at the water and, in their mind, stepped away from themselves, or at least stepped towards the water. The cheap plastic chair indicates a site from which a person has observed the water and, if not enjoyed it, then listened to it, possibly even entertaining the notion that the water was listening to them, or something along those lines. What the plastic chair theory says to me is that if we are to reframe our relationship with nature, as we desperately need to do, then we had best do it close to home. Rather than travel to a National Park, you would be better off following the flow of your sewer to where it runs into a stream, a point at which there is less likely to be a fancy park and more likely to be a cheap plastic chair, or sometimes just a big rock to sit on, a satisfactory alternative.

My theory is just a theory, of course. How can I prove a point of human interaction? Where is the fact when the human mind connects with the mind of the world? But if I were to attempt to write up my theory and submit it to a major scientific journal, I would use, in lieu of charts and graphs, these photographs by Nicholas Pollack, which along with proving my theory (if only for me) are wonderful evocations of what it is like to love the Meadowlands. In these photos you feel the wide-open sky that is the centerpiece of the Meadowlands experience. You sense what seems inexhaustibly pastoral as you simultaneously see the apparatus of the energy industry that exhausts it: sometimes the smoke from the Essex County incinerator stands out, a plume of white gray; sometimes it mingles with the low gray sky. The delicate creams and tans in these lovely plates make the green of the meadows a palpable shock, as if emphasizing the vitality of the place that is nearly but not strangled by impoundments and extensions, by development that never lets up. In the place and in these portraits, persistence and resistance are the themes.

For this little community of friends that Pollack has portrayed so kindly, the tracks and tunnels and truck yards make the place a refuge from a relentless and impersonal world, from our day-to-day existence that sometimes seems to only get better at impersonating a life that's alive and connected. I am reminded of the videos made by pilots with the National Oceanic and Atmospheric Administration, who fly through the terrifying turbulence of a hurricane only to arrive at last at the eye of the storm, peaceful and clear, the turbulence in even greater perspective on the pilots' return. Pollack's pictures of beers and cards, of strong coffee and dominoes remind us that community is as rare as the most endangered plants. They point us to a truth that is increasingly overgrown with buzzwords (green, sustainable, resilient), terms that might have been first employed with change in mind but have since become sanitized and invasive themselves in the way corporations have branded them. In the process, our language and digital addictions have diluted our sense of self and place, diverting us from taking our place in the plastic chair.

For if we are to reimagine the way we live with the world—because the way we are living now is destroying the world and us in the meantime—then it begins with deepening our awareness of each other, of the people we live with, all of them. It's selfishness that's invasive; weeds are only what separates us from others and the larger world. Henry David Thoreau would have liked the guys that Nicholas Pollack has photographed, the crew who invited this photographer in. If you are at all shocked by me saying this then you only know the fancy Thoreau, the one who worked for Emerson and is today quoted in environment-friendly advertisements or disparaged by an aggressive strain of eco-aesthetes. You don't know the Thoreau whose father ran the store in the center of Concord, Massachusetts, the sort of place that today in Jersey City or Secaucus you might call a bodega. Thoreau would love these guys not because they set up a shack on the edge of town. But because they made a little community at the center of the world.

Robert Sullivan

2021

What is a 'meadow'? A meadow is in part a seminary, a seed-bed, not a climax ecosystem but a set of resilient potentialities for new life and new life-networks. Maybe there's an audio-synchrony here between 'meadow' and 'middle', as in the 'middle of nowhere' which is where Nicholas Pollack's vision takes us and loses us and lets us rest and reflect. 'Nowhere', in turn, can be retranslated, via Sir Thomas More and Plato, to its Greek linguistic origins, as 'utopia'. The 'middle of nowhere' where Nicholas Pollack takes us is a 'meadow of utopia'— not a perfected social or natural habitat, but an ordinary, largely neglected, place in the world where ordinary, seemingly castoff people can find themselves at home, as the fast and ambitious world passes by, too much in a hurry to even notice or care that they could be as much at home there as the geese and the rabbits and the sparrows and blackbirds and rats and cats, and where the refuse and bric-a-brac might just be milestones revealing, if they bothered to notice, that what was once castoff might just come to be again, all the more precious because of its seeming worthlessness. William Carlos Williams, New Jersey's greatest modernist poet, concludes his harsh but tender poem 'To Elsie' with a kind of epiphany:

'It is only in isolate flecks that
something
is given off

No one
to witness
and adjust, no one to drive the car'.

In *Meadow*, Nicholas Pollack responds to the poet, becomes the witness and drives the car, and shares his witness with us, opening our eyes to see and to share, momentarily and gratefully, in that subliminal something given off; and just maybe, in those isolate flecks from the middle of nowhere, we do find ourselves.

William Shullenberger

The meadow, a patch of grass near a stream where sheep can graze, evokes the pastoral, which is not an image or sentiment known to the native Chinese, whose civilization is based on pigs and chickens raised in barns. To think that if I had never left China, no matter how many Chinese poems I read, I wouldn't have come across a landscape that poets like Shakespeare, Milton, and Wordsworth celebrated. But whether the celebration be Milton's "Meadows trim, with daisies pied" or Wordsworth's meadow that, to him as a child, was clothed in "celestial light," they are not the only ways to understand and appreciate what is, realistically, just a patch of grass. How far its meaning can be extended is superbly demonstrated in Nicholas Pollack's images. So I sincerely recommend that you who happen upon this book closely attend, learn from, and enjoy the somber beauty of its photos. You might perhaps expect beauty in an art book, but what you may not expect is that Pollack can also persuade you to see the ordinary meadow as a place of generous hospitality and friendship.

Yi-Fu Tuan

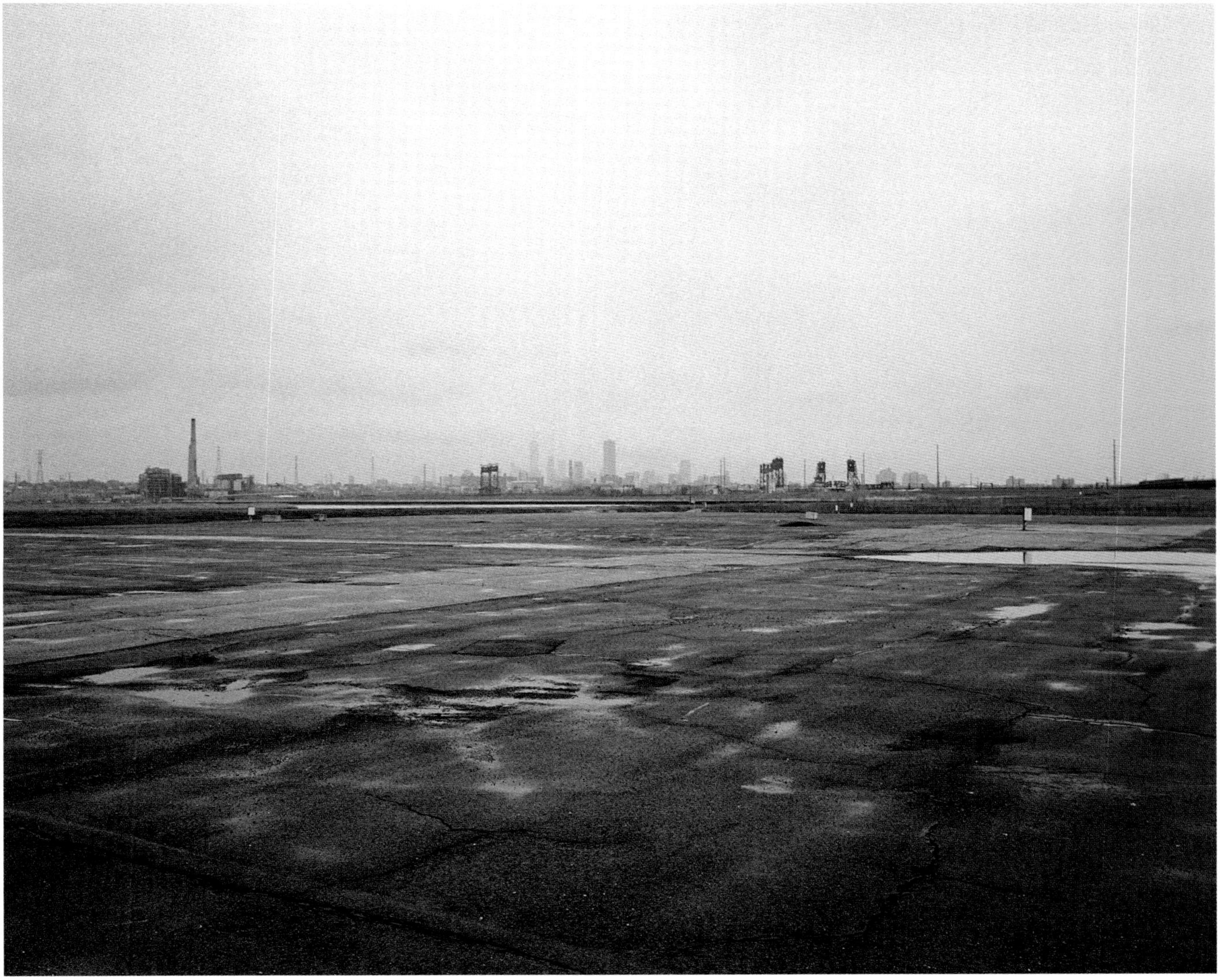

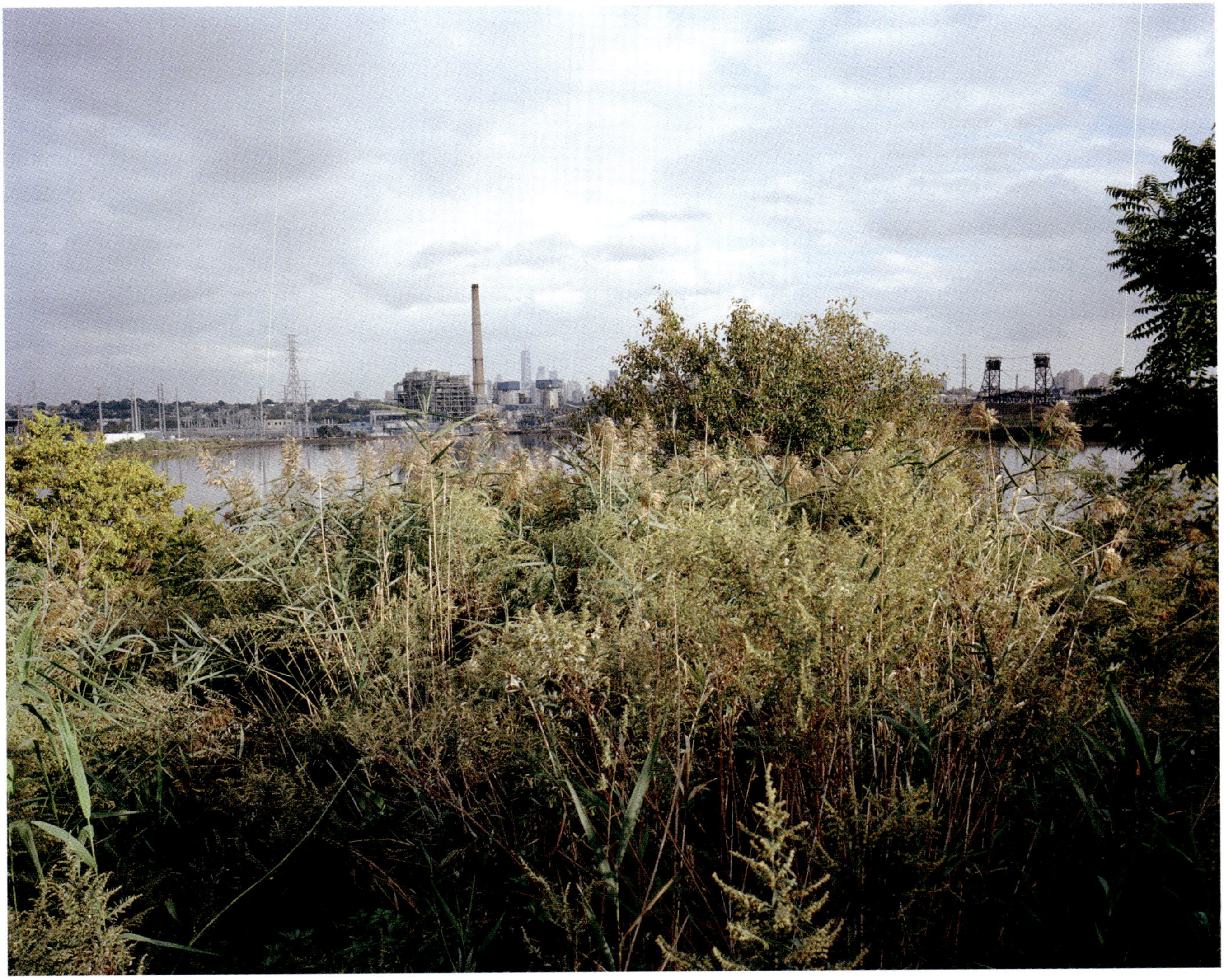

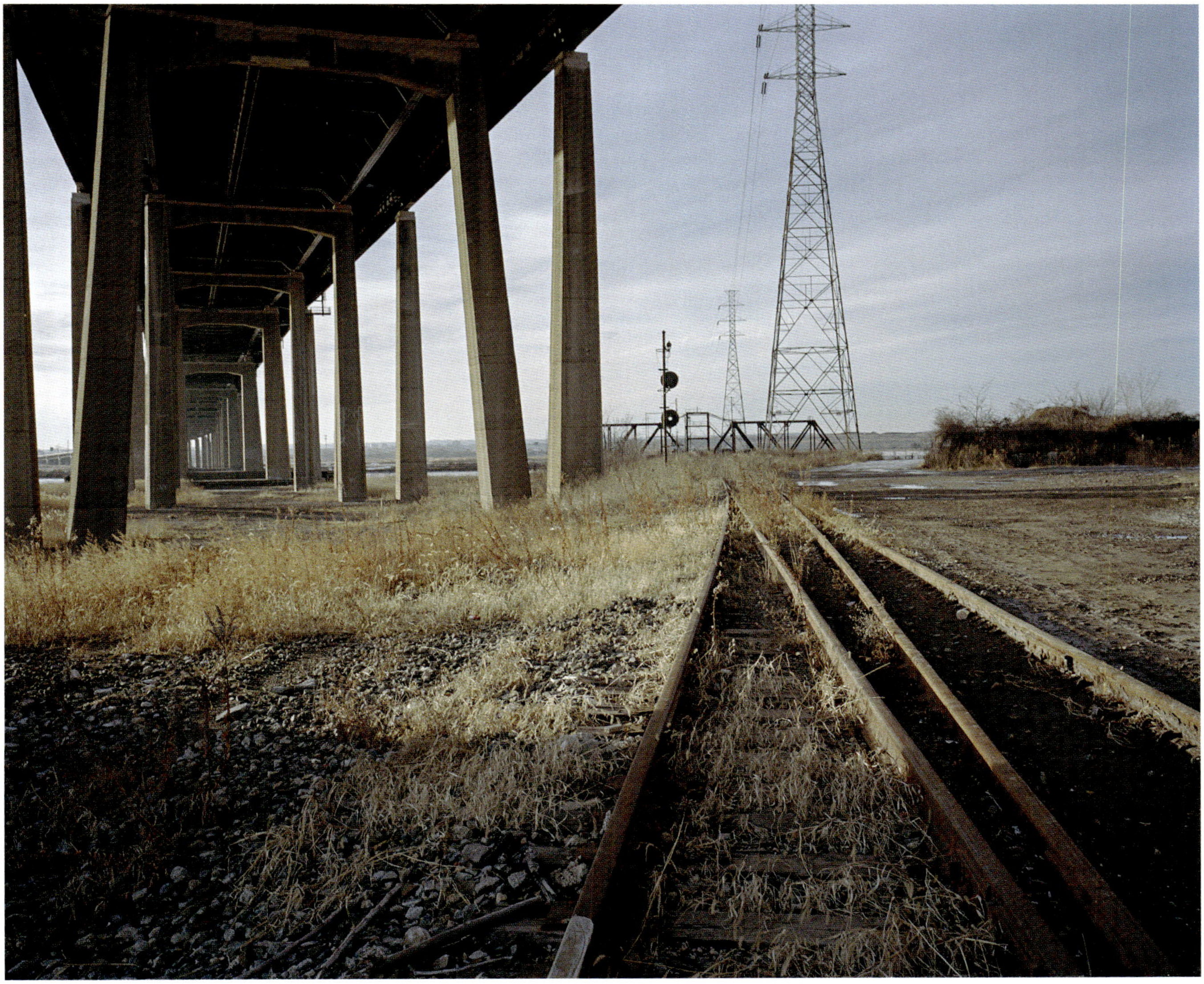

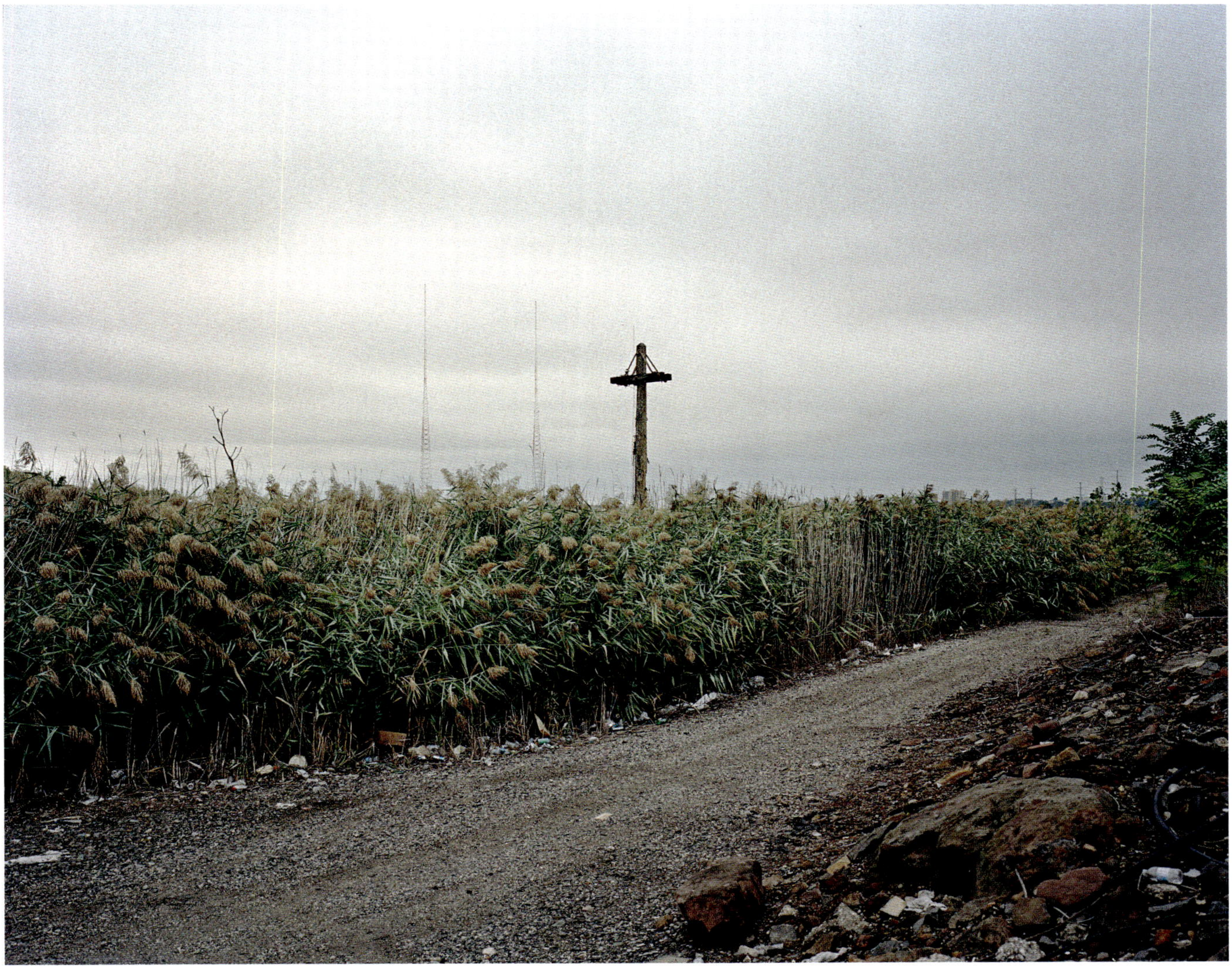

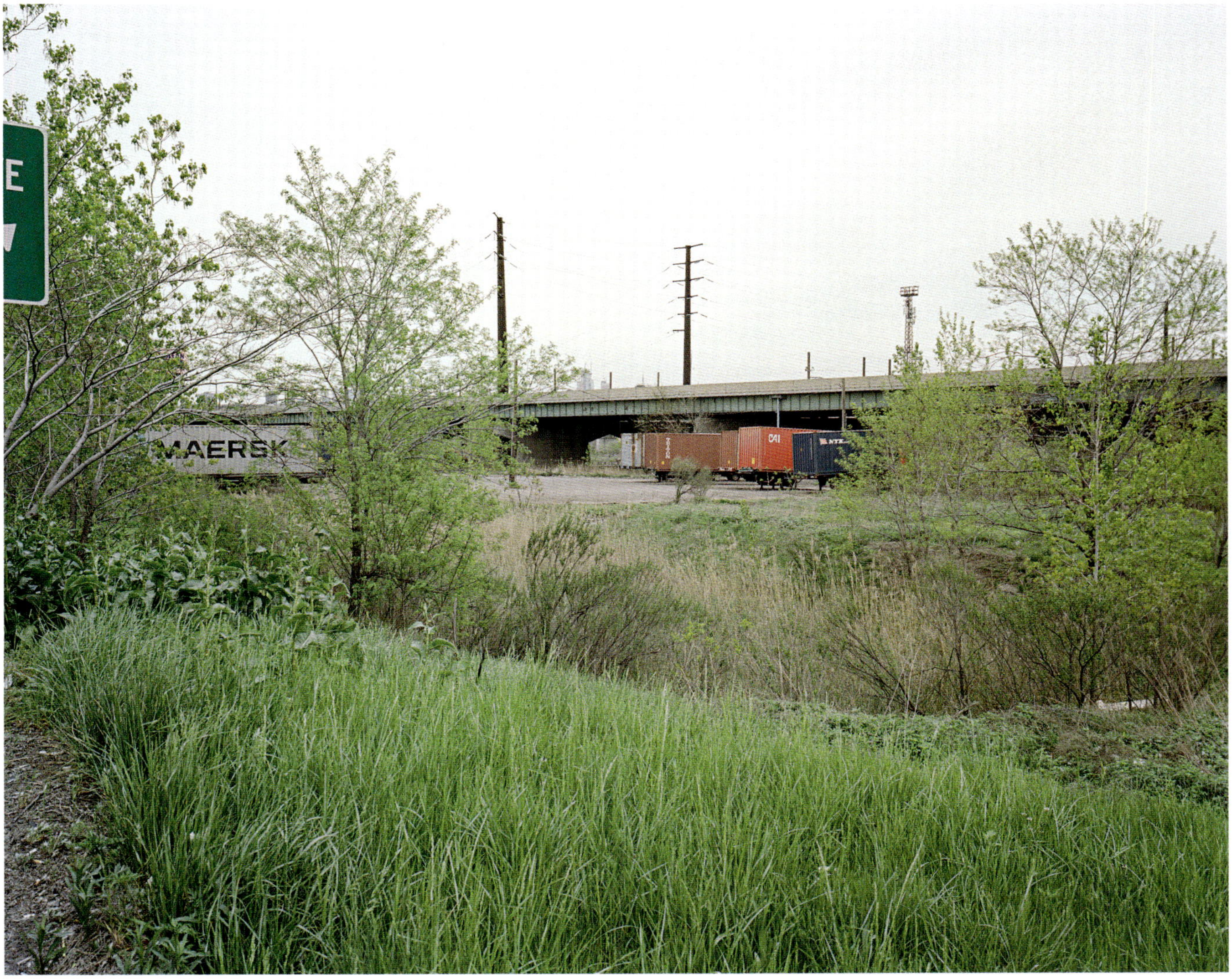
MAERSK

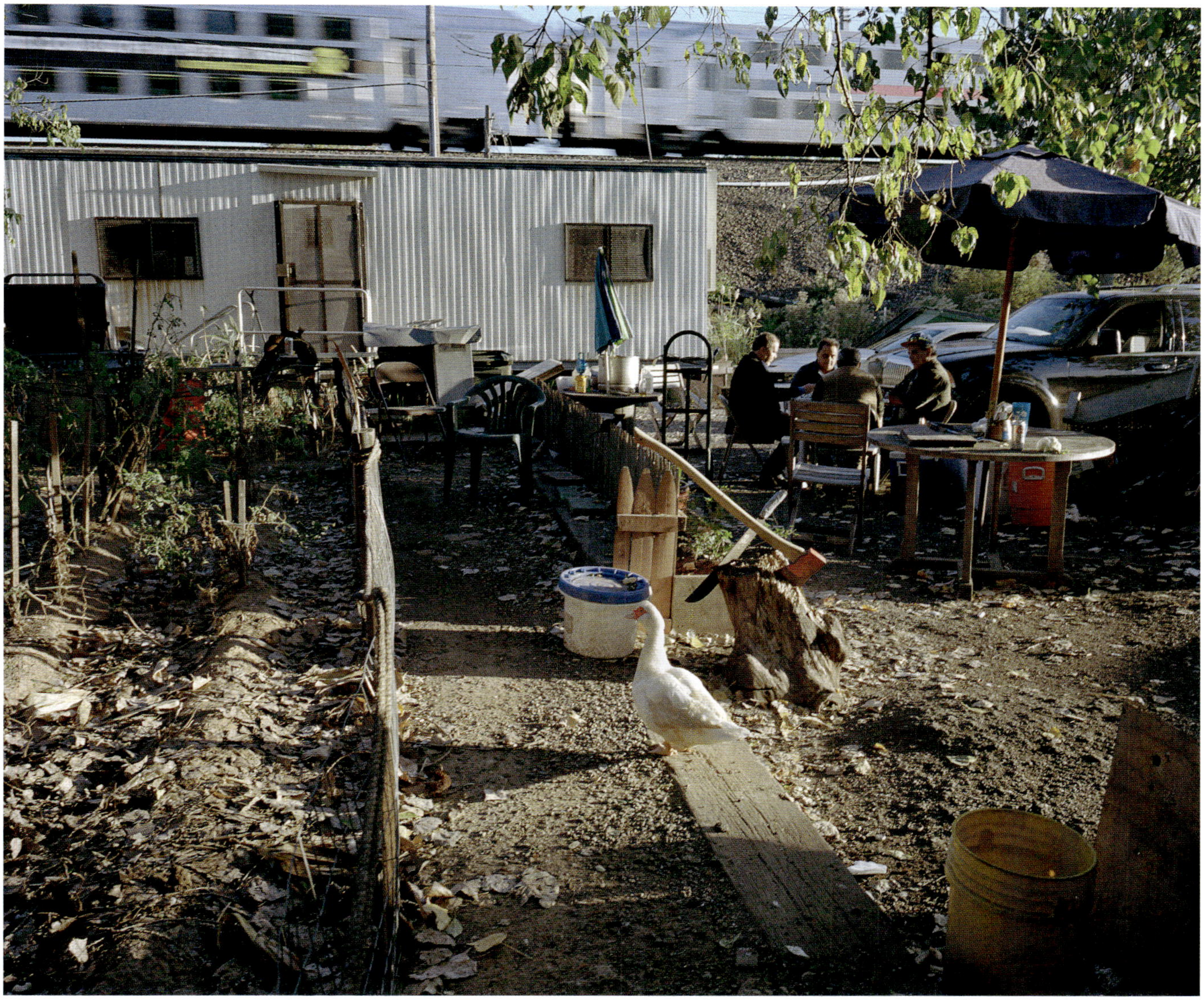

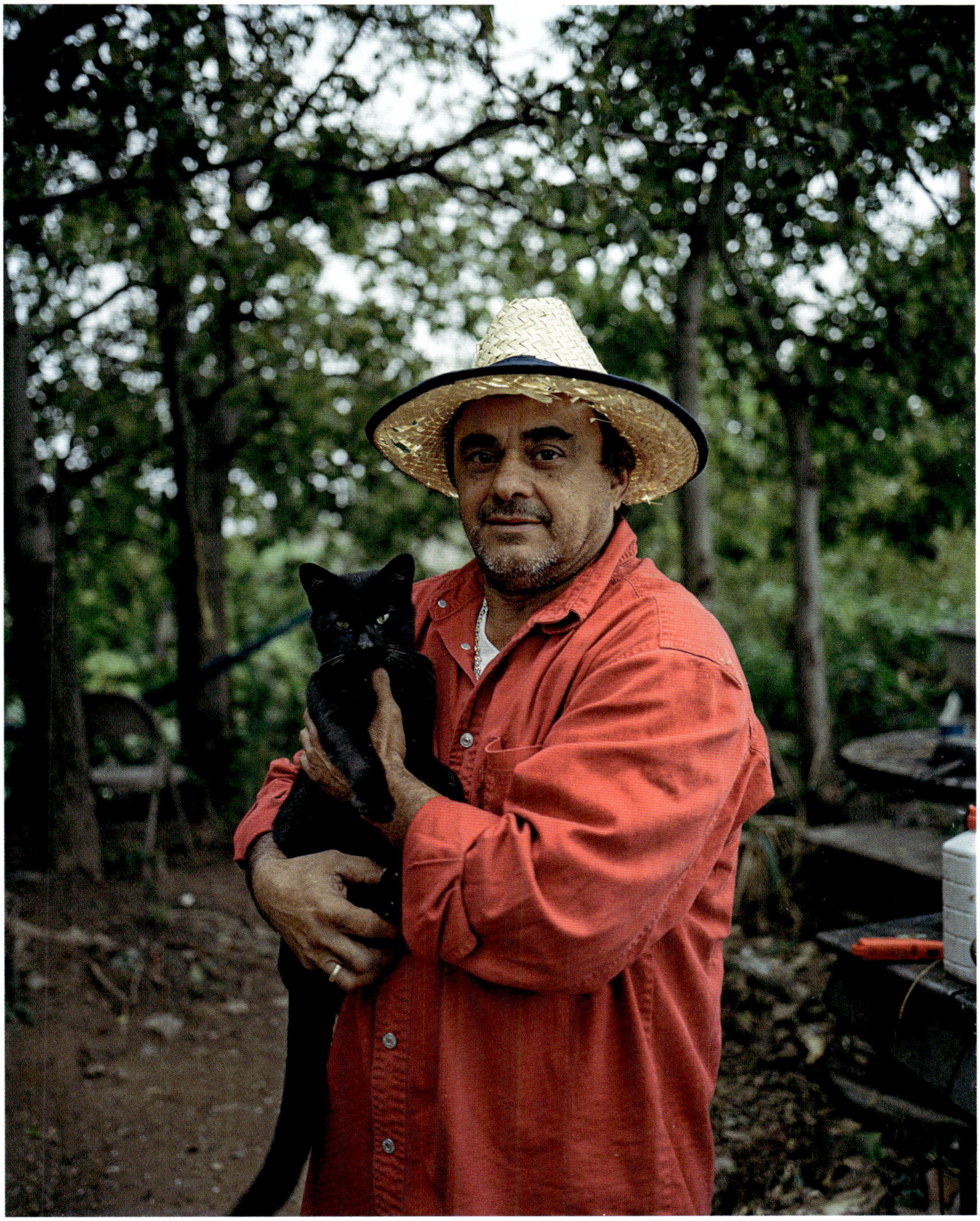

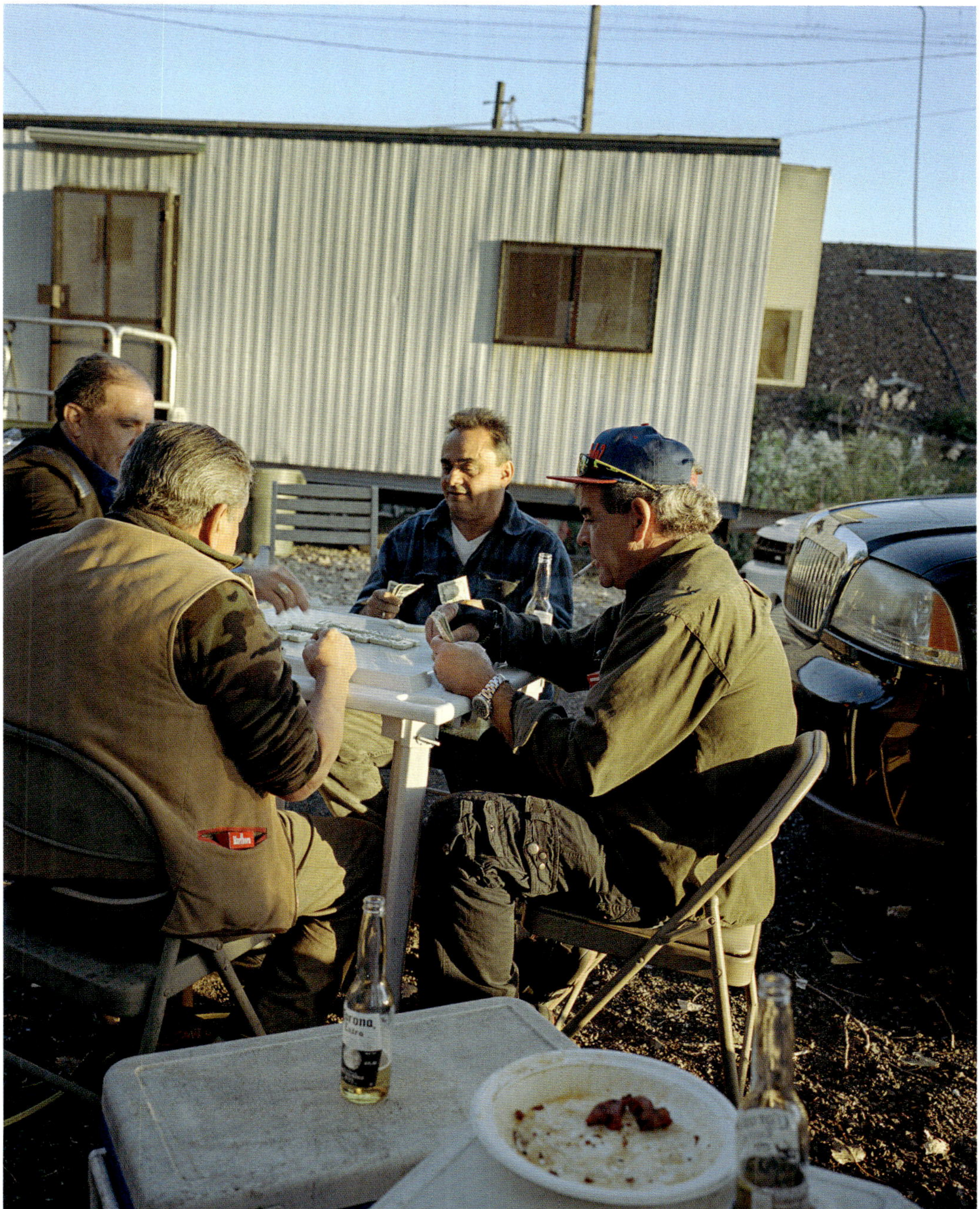

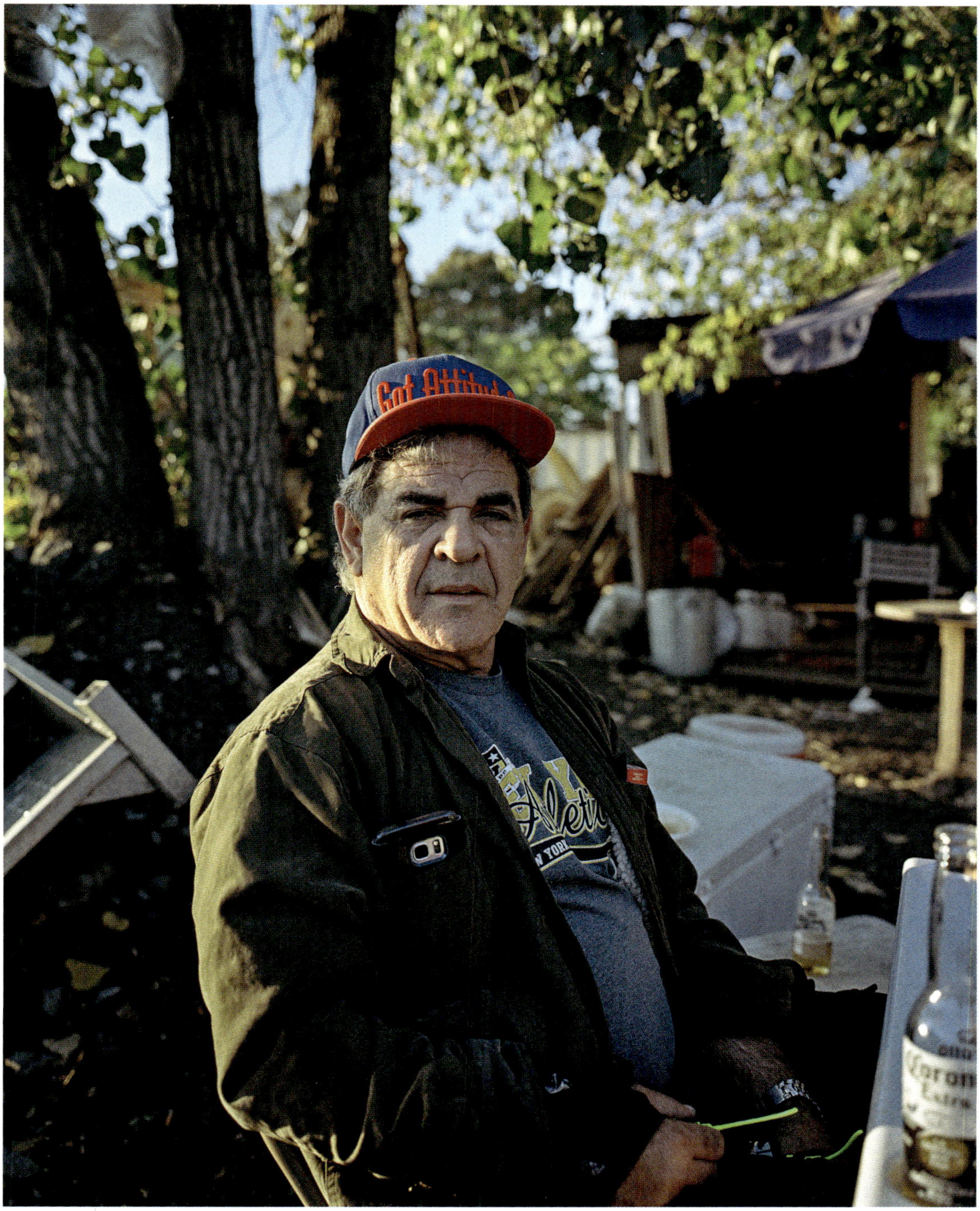

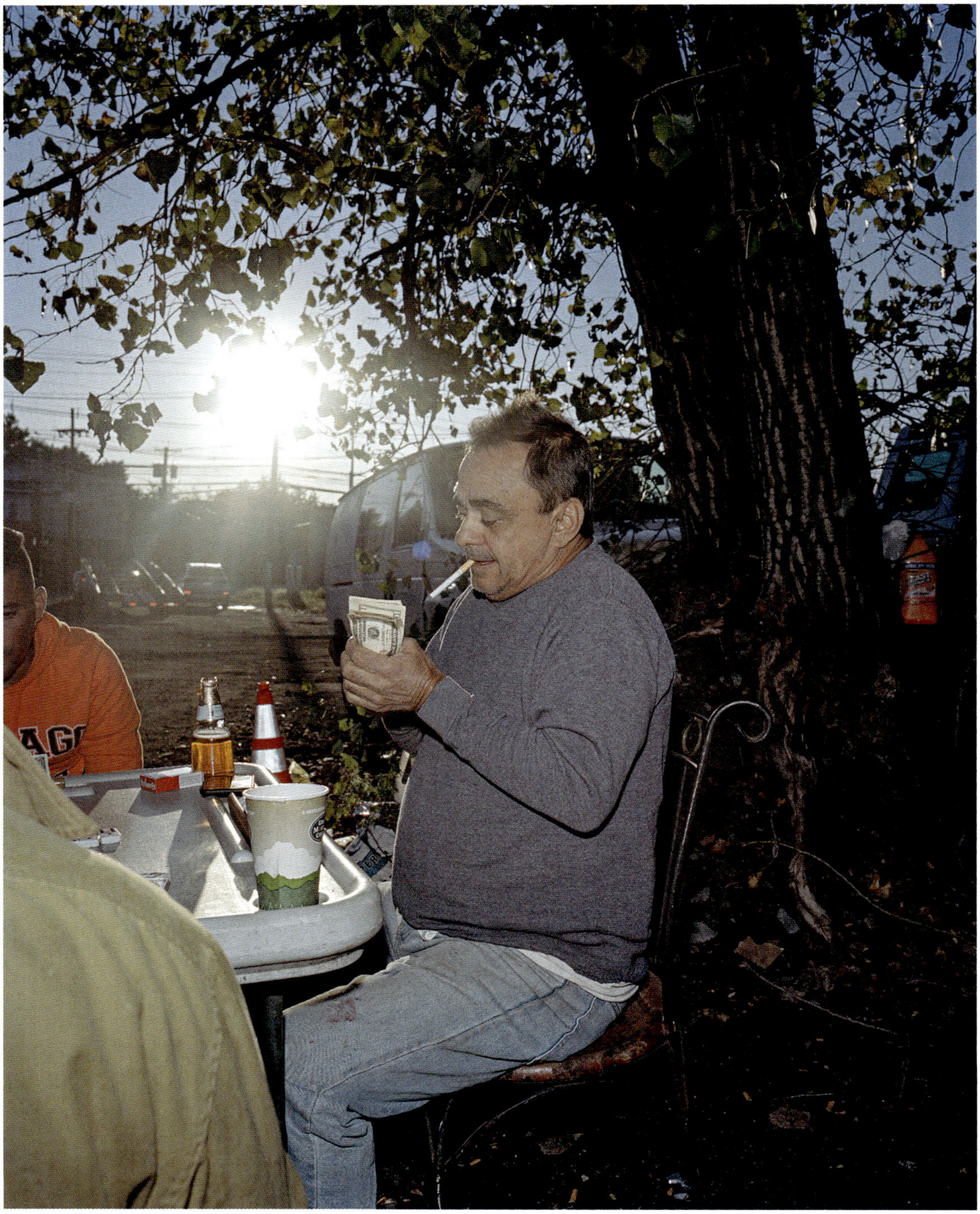

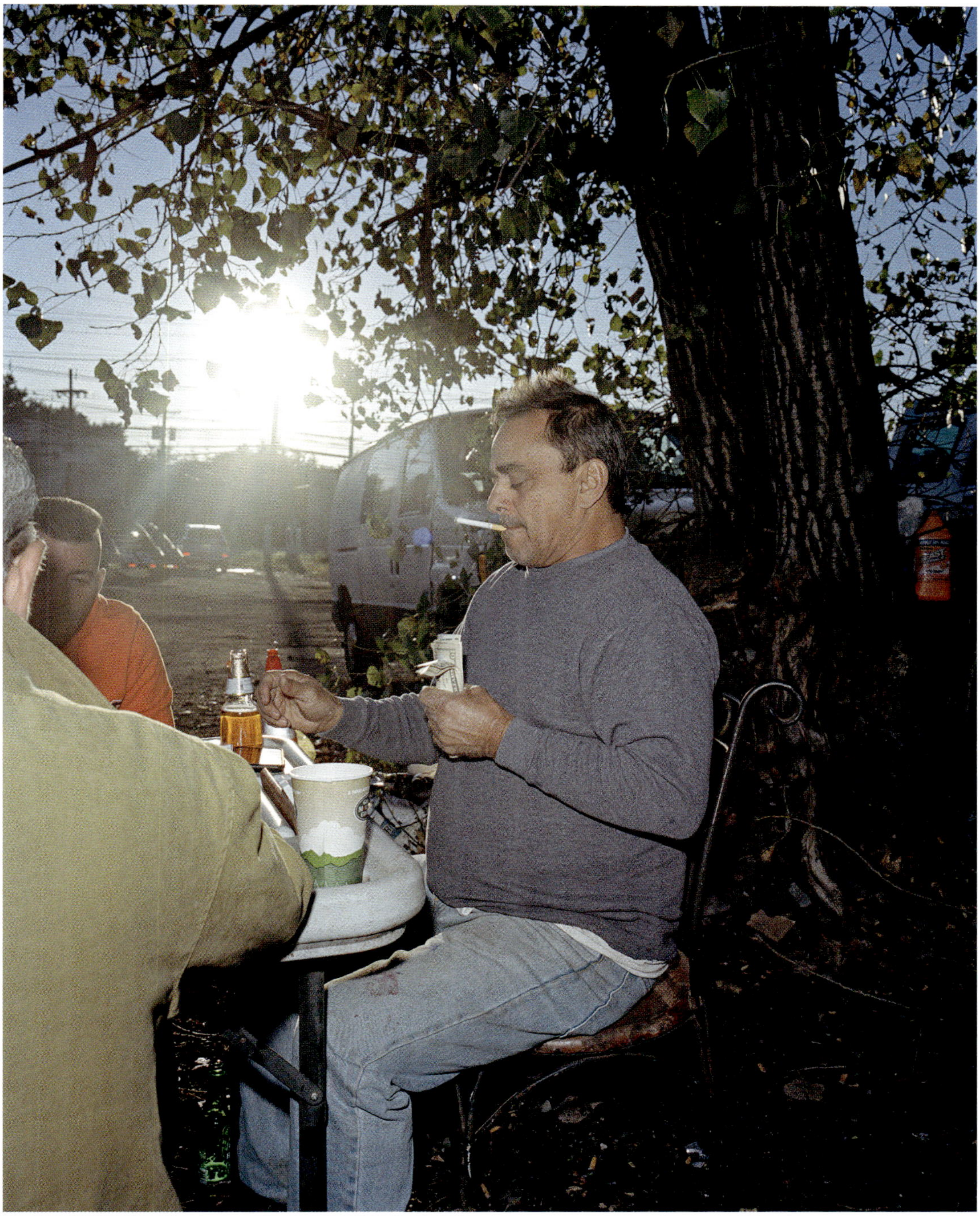

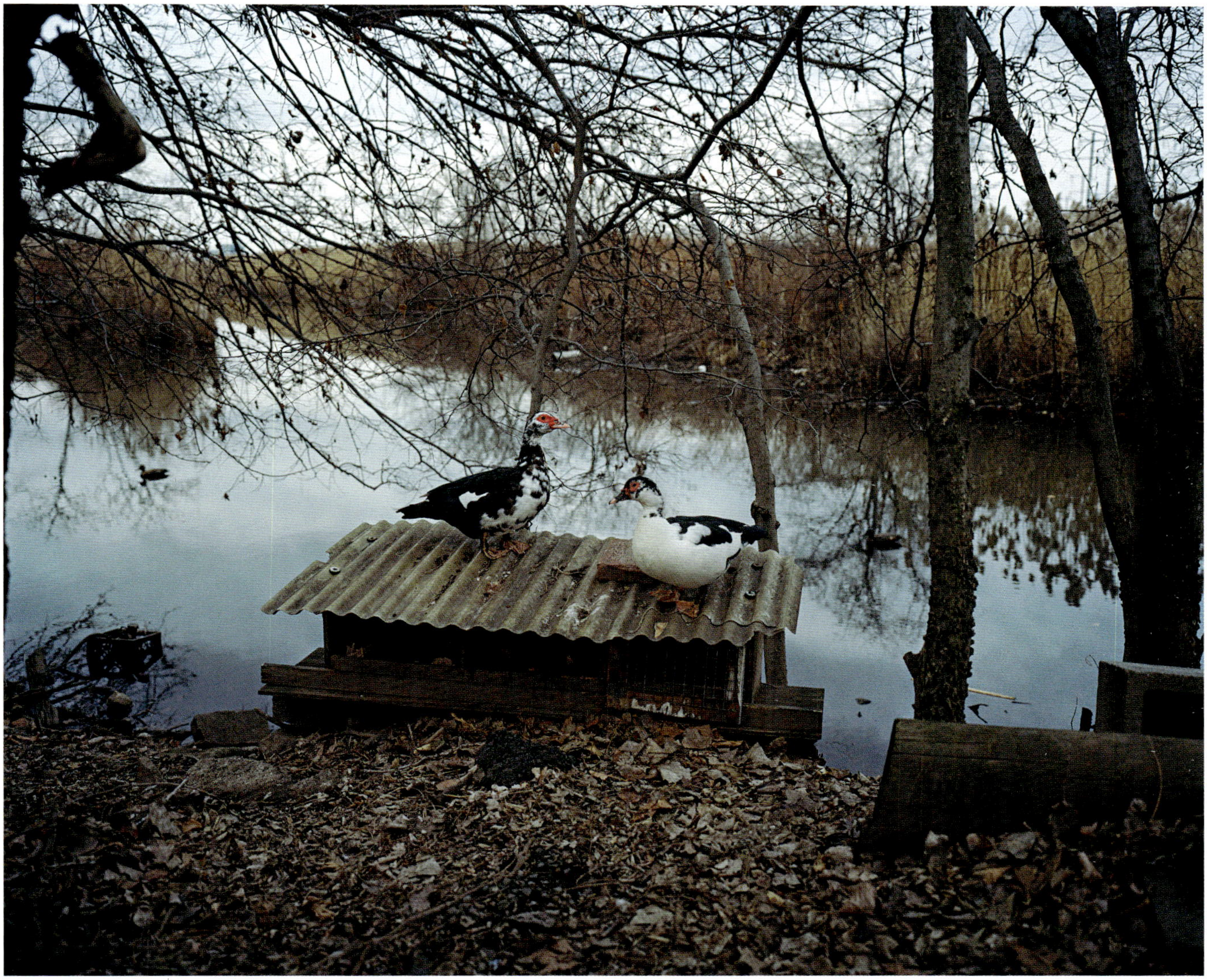

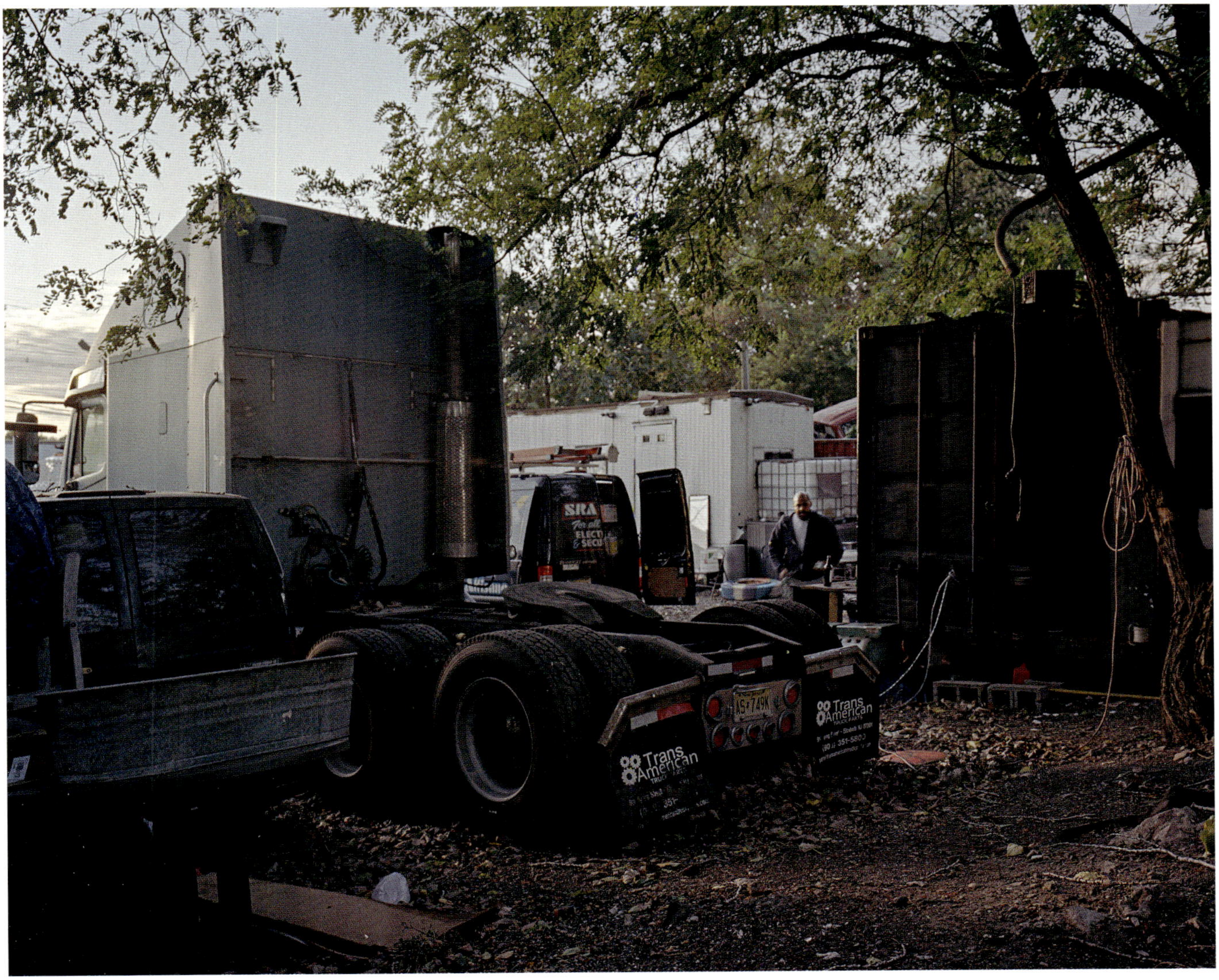
SRA
Trans American
Trans American

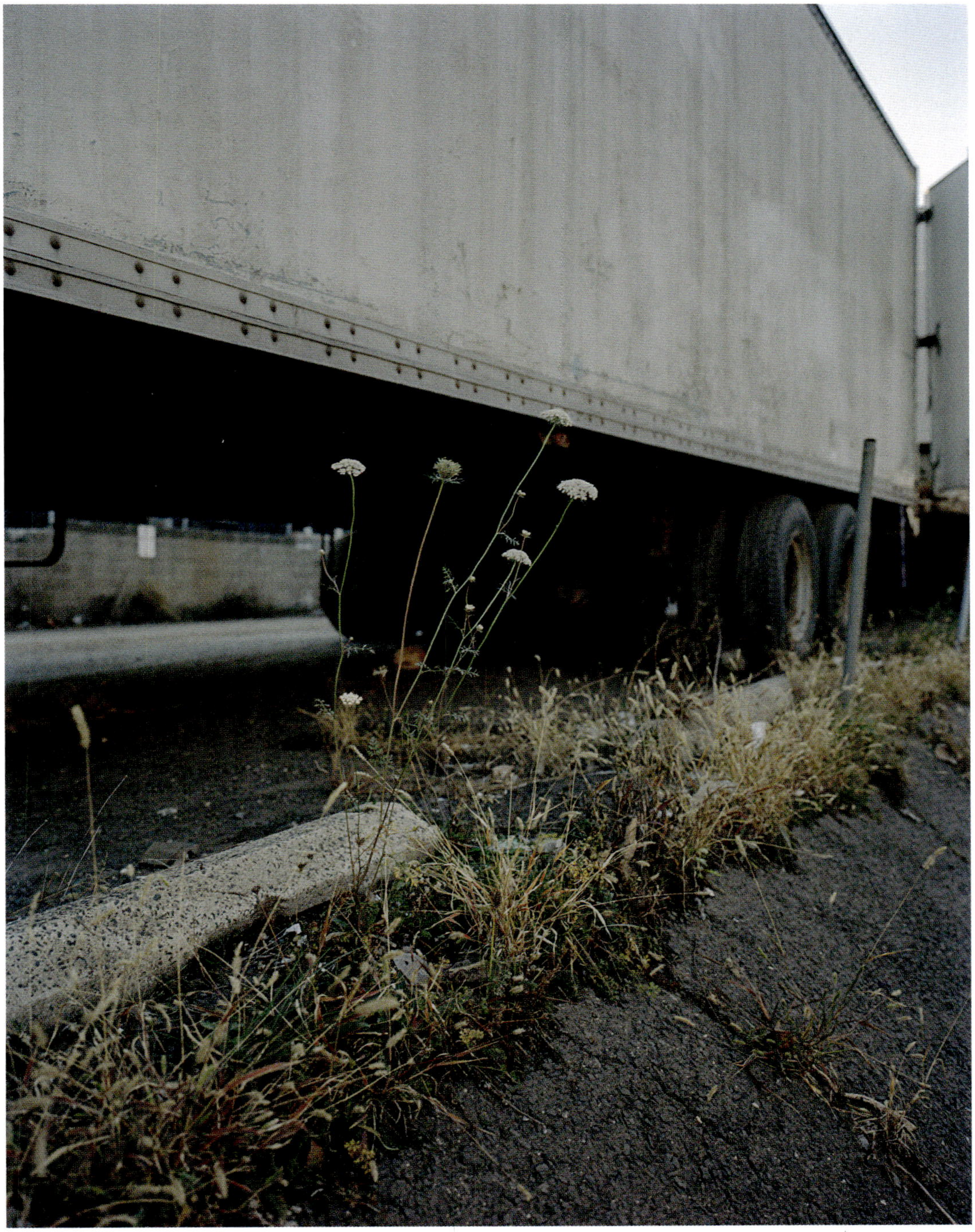

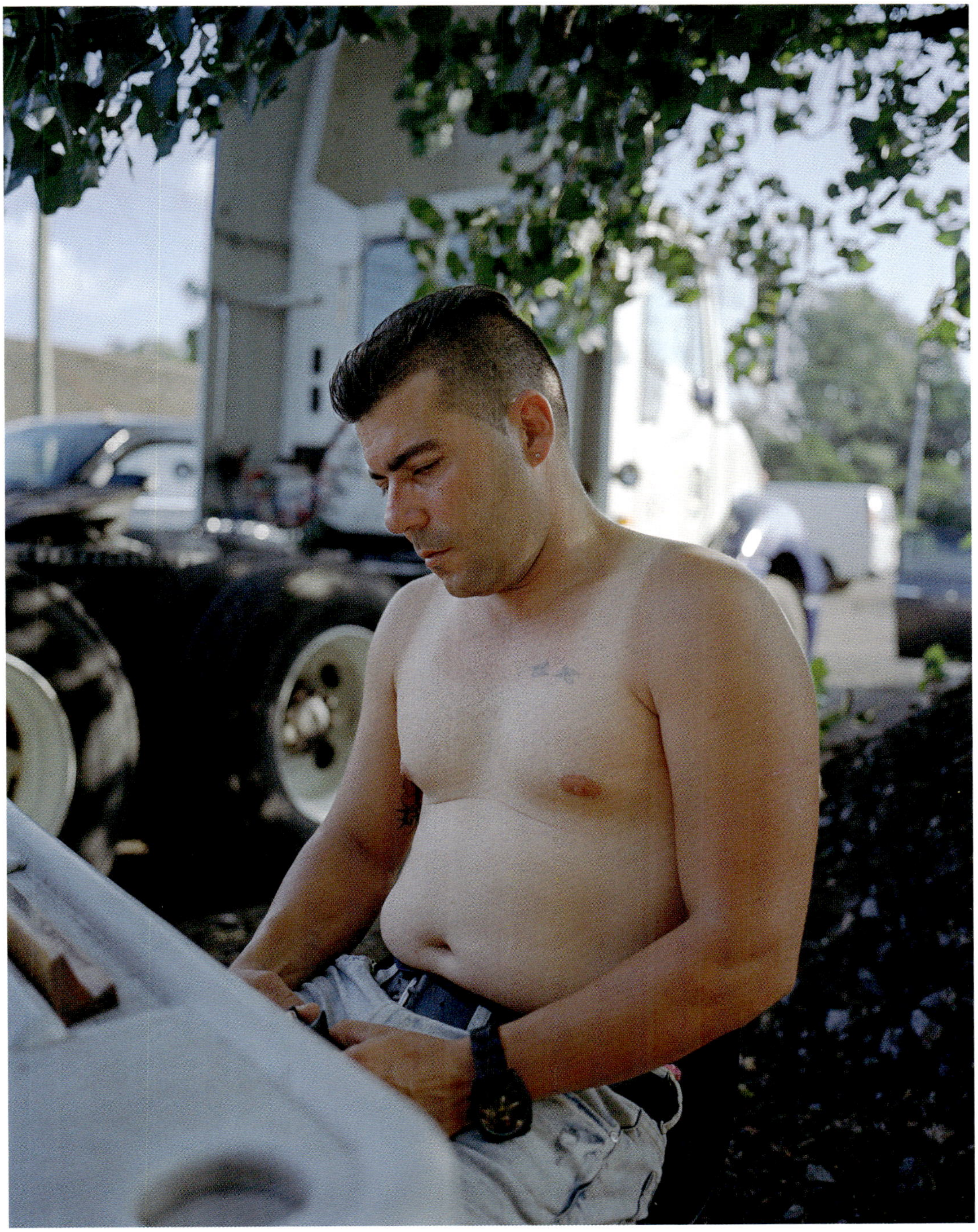

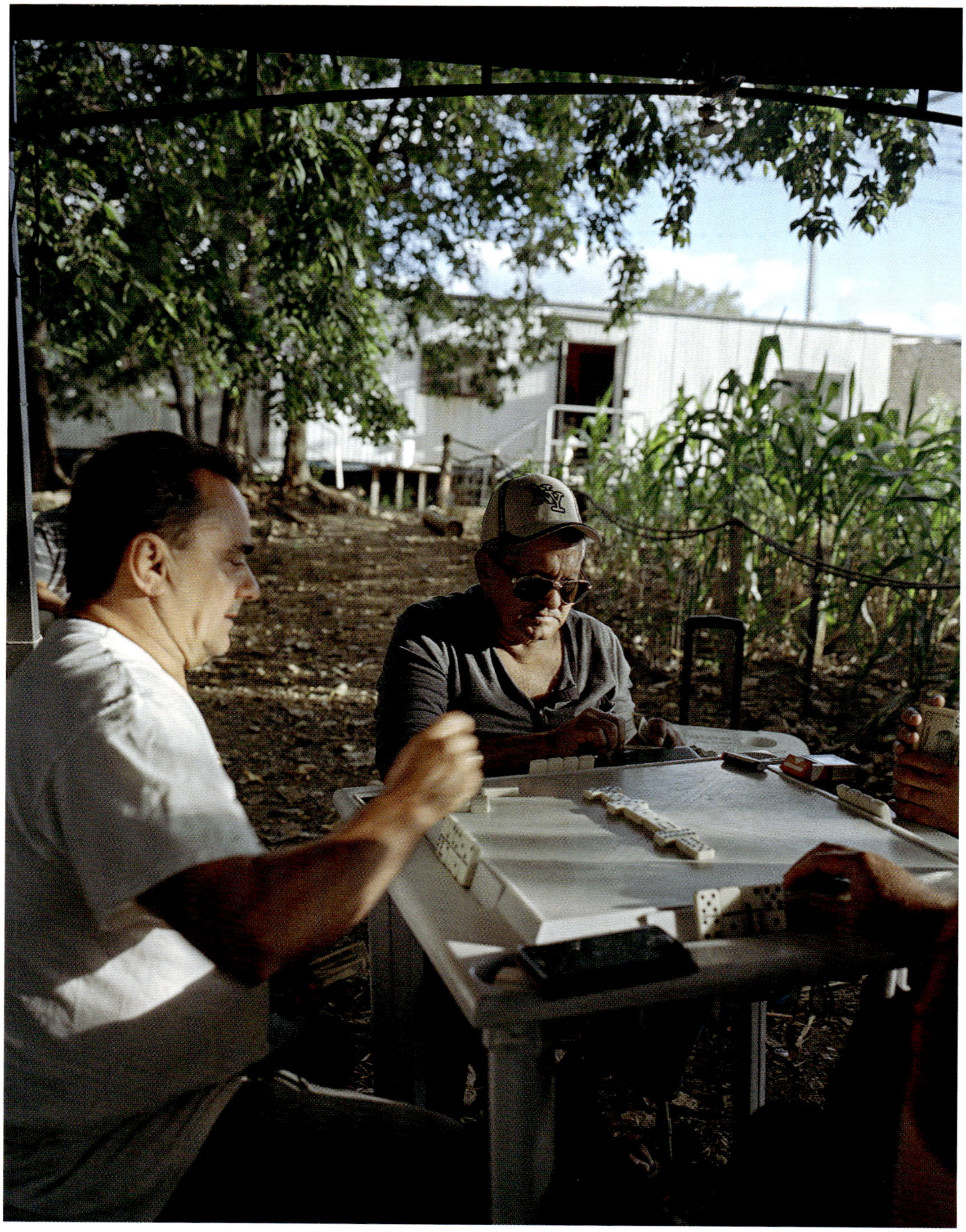

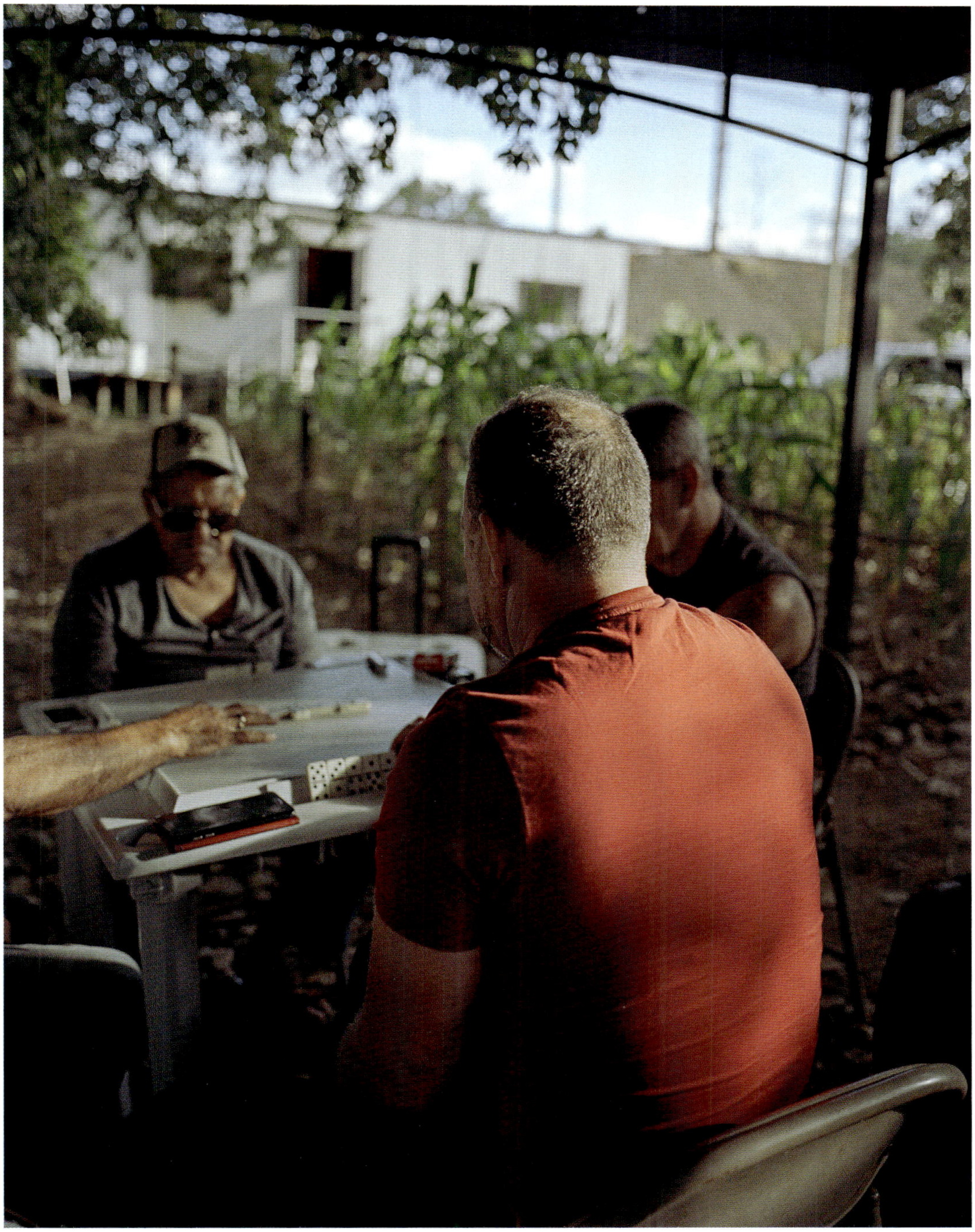

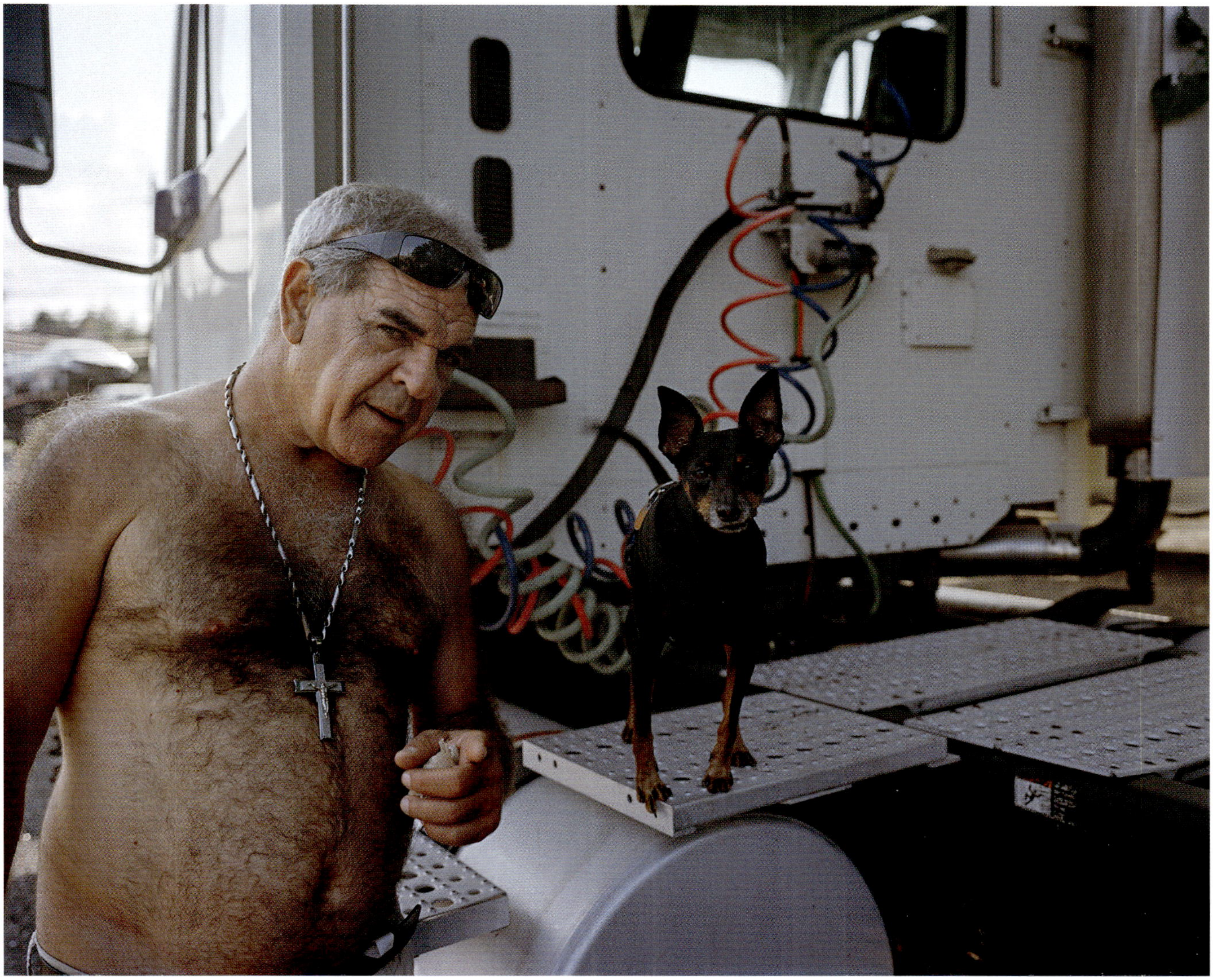

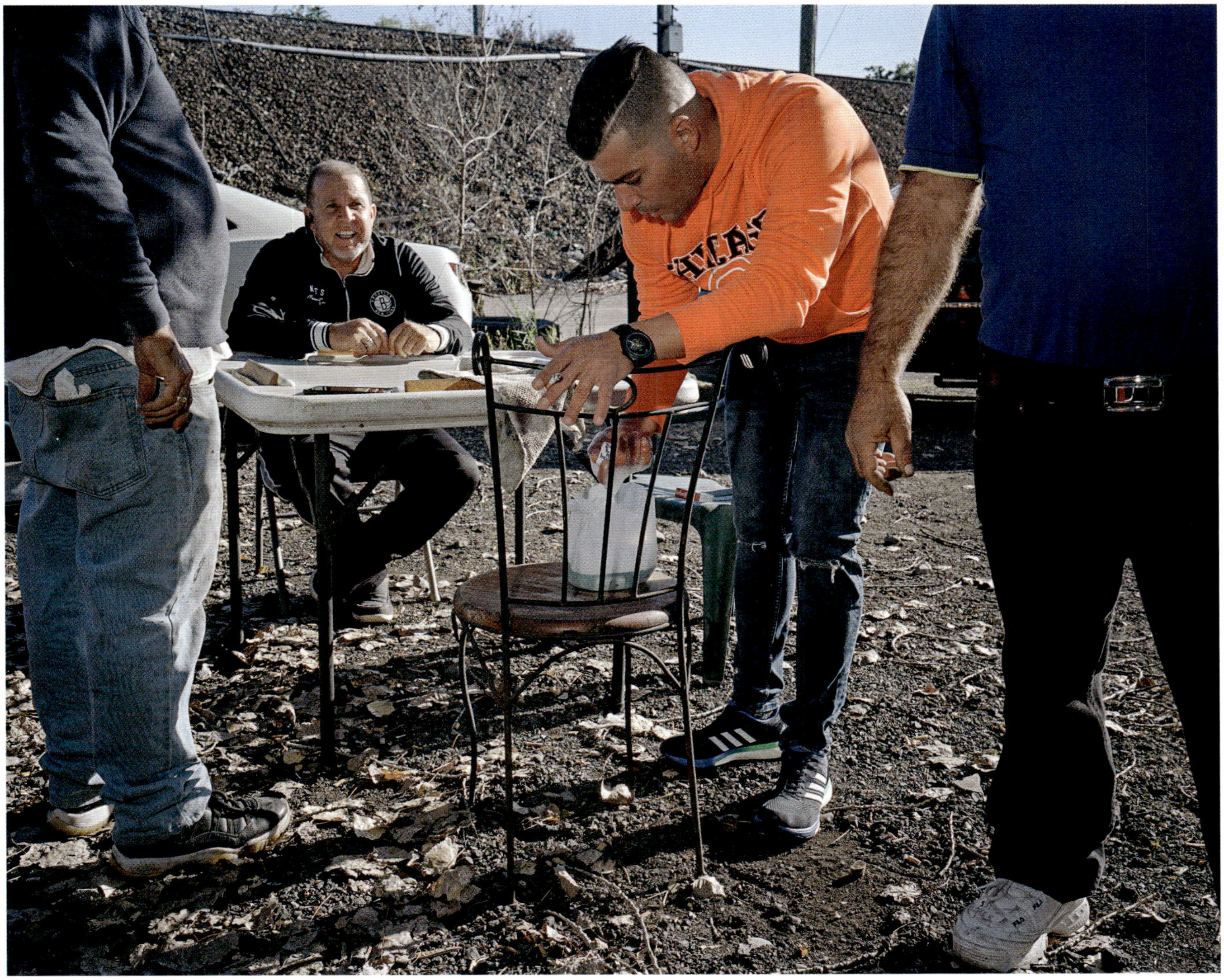

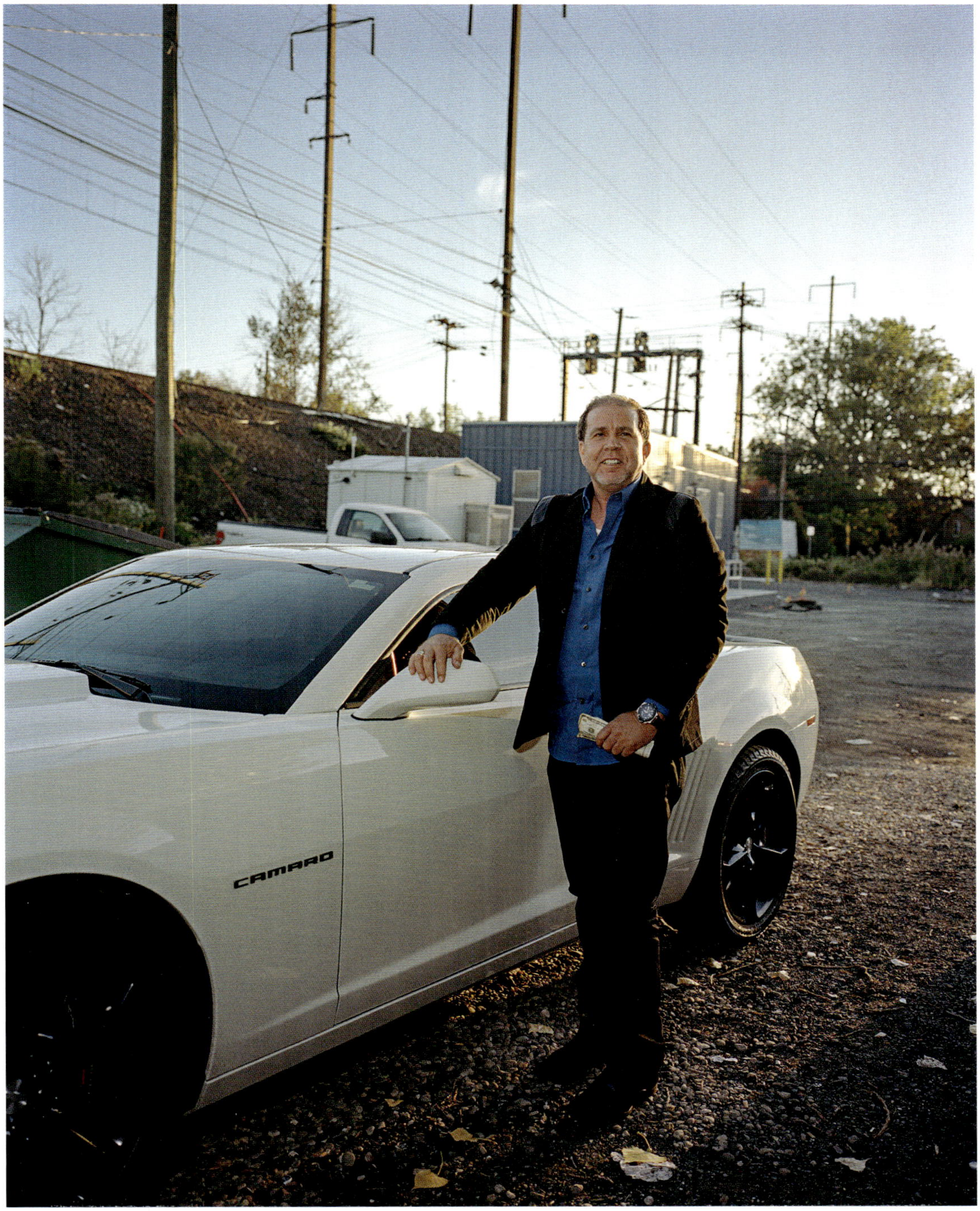
CAMARO

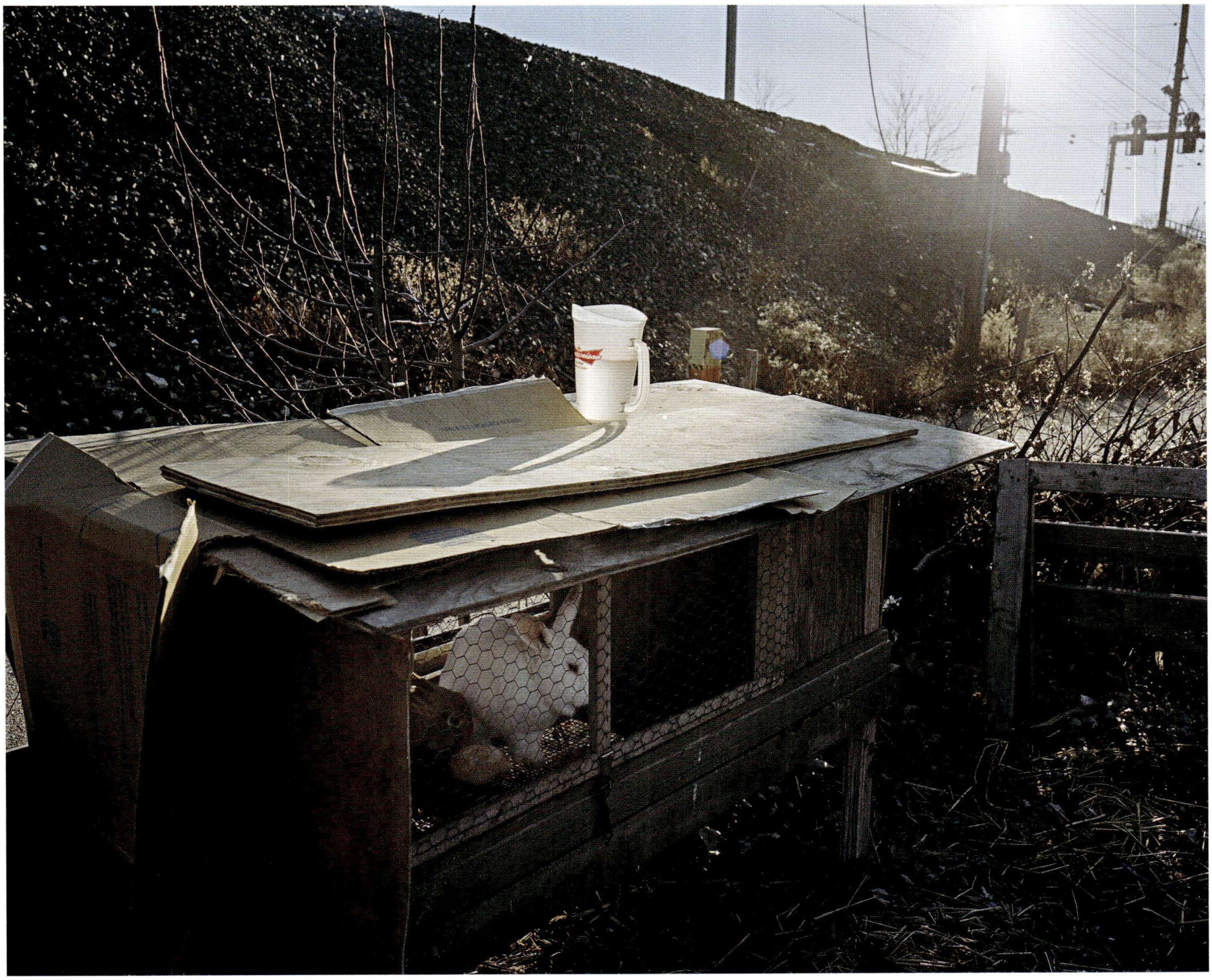

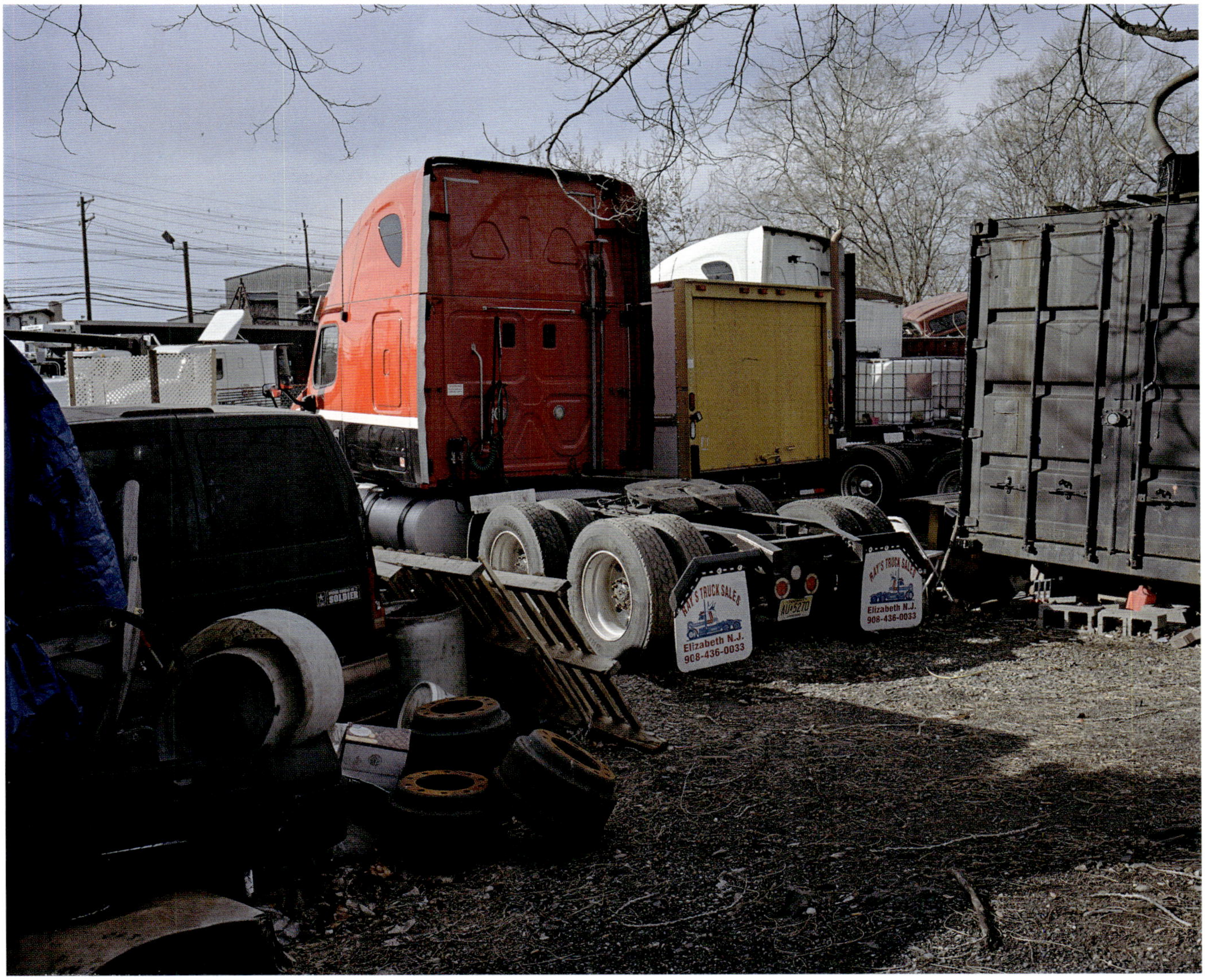
SOLDIER
RAY'S TRUCK SALES
Elizabeth N.J.
908-436-0033
RAY'S TRUCK SALES
Elizabeth N.J.
908-436-0033

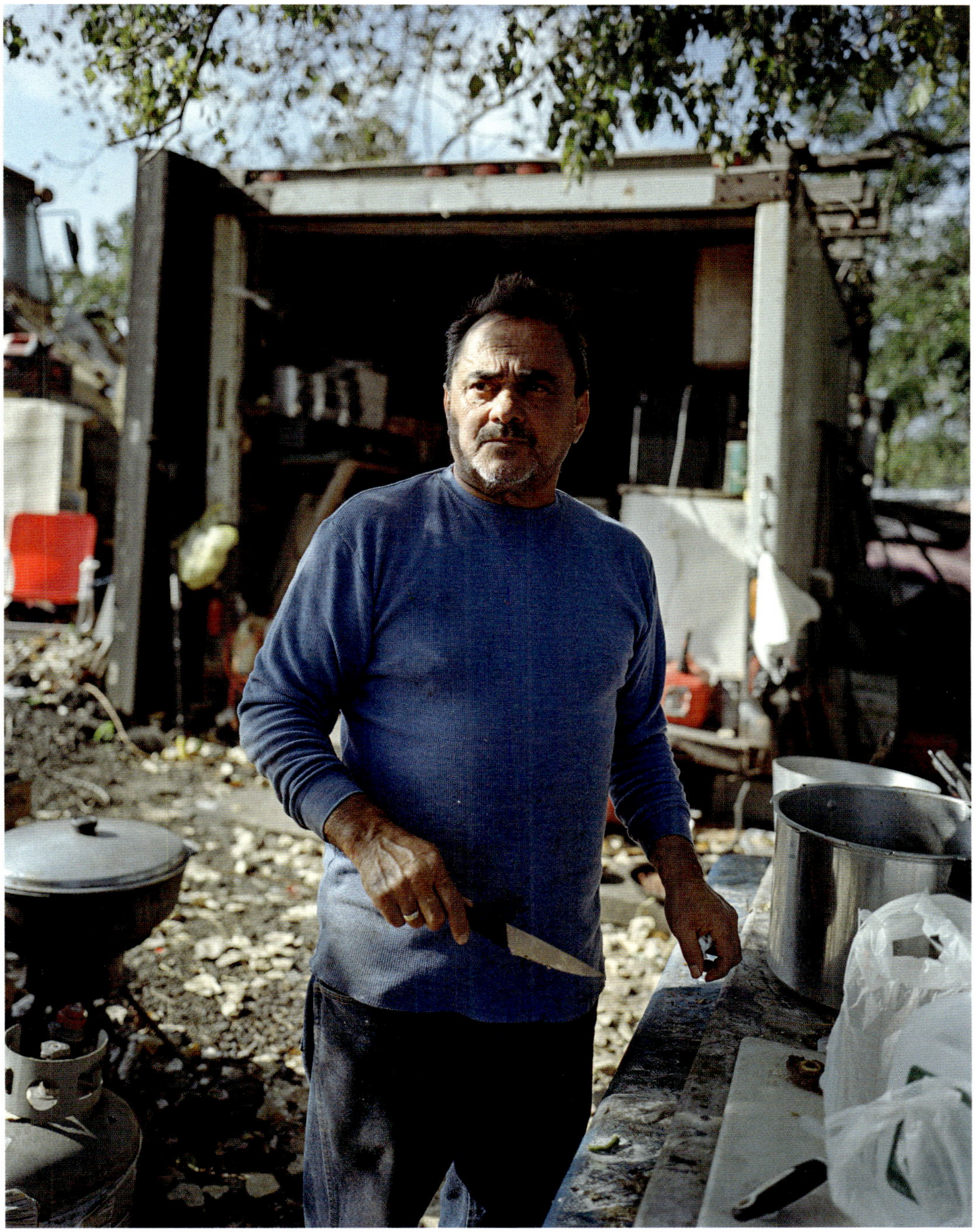

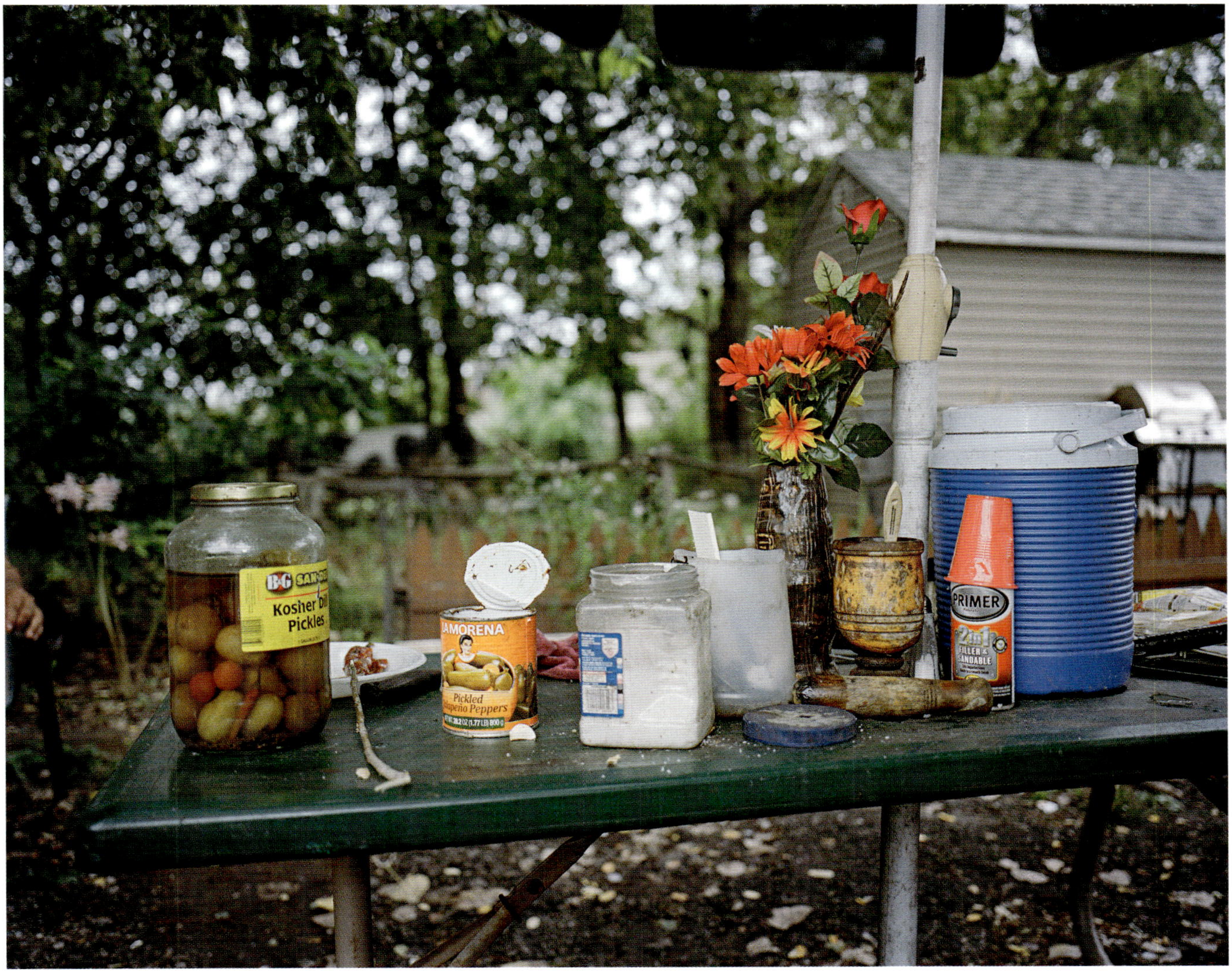
B&G
Kosher Dil
Pickles
LA MORENA
Pickled
PRIMER
2in1
FILLER &
SANDABLE

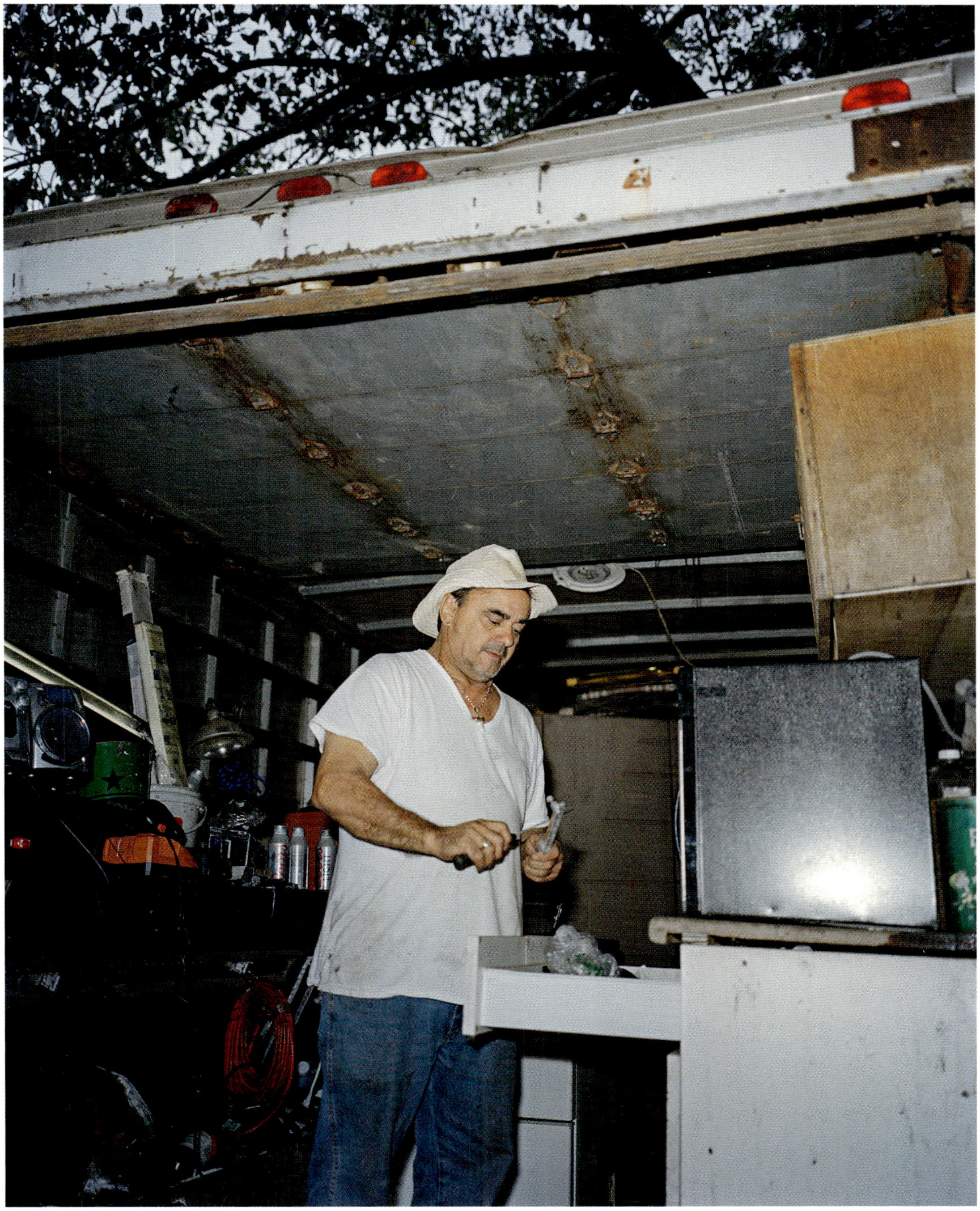

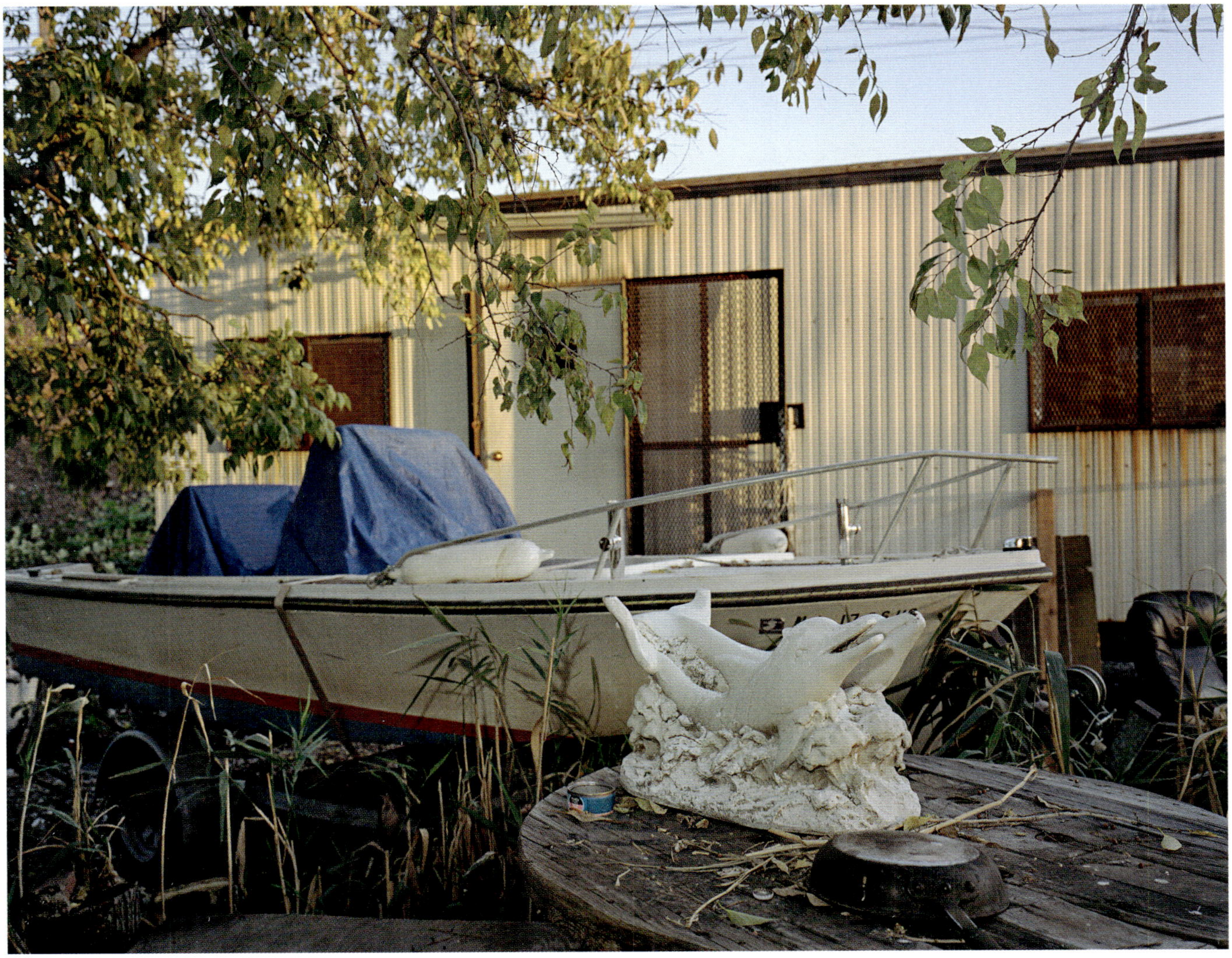

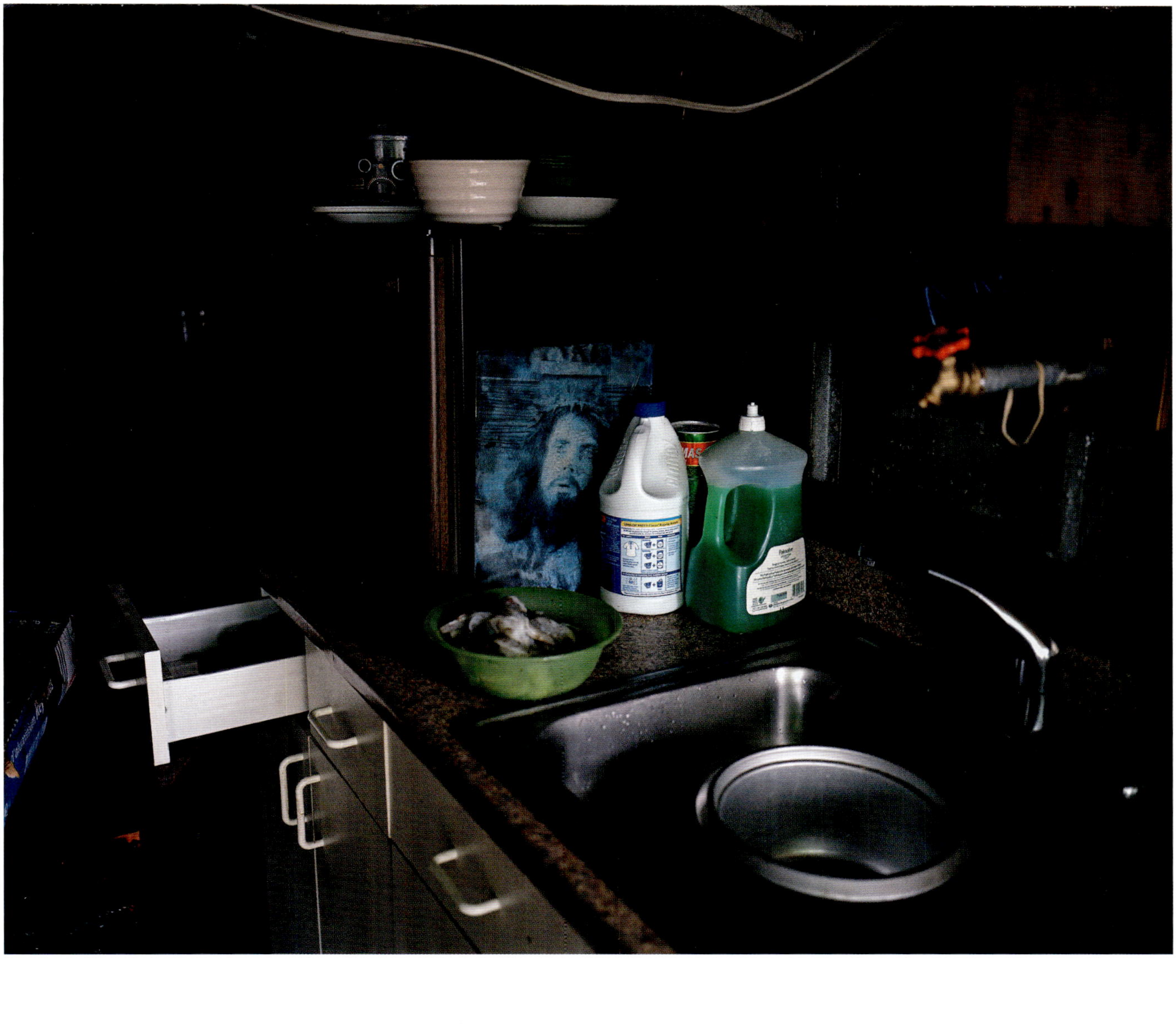

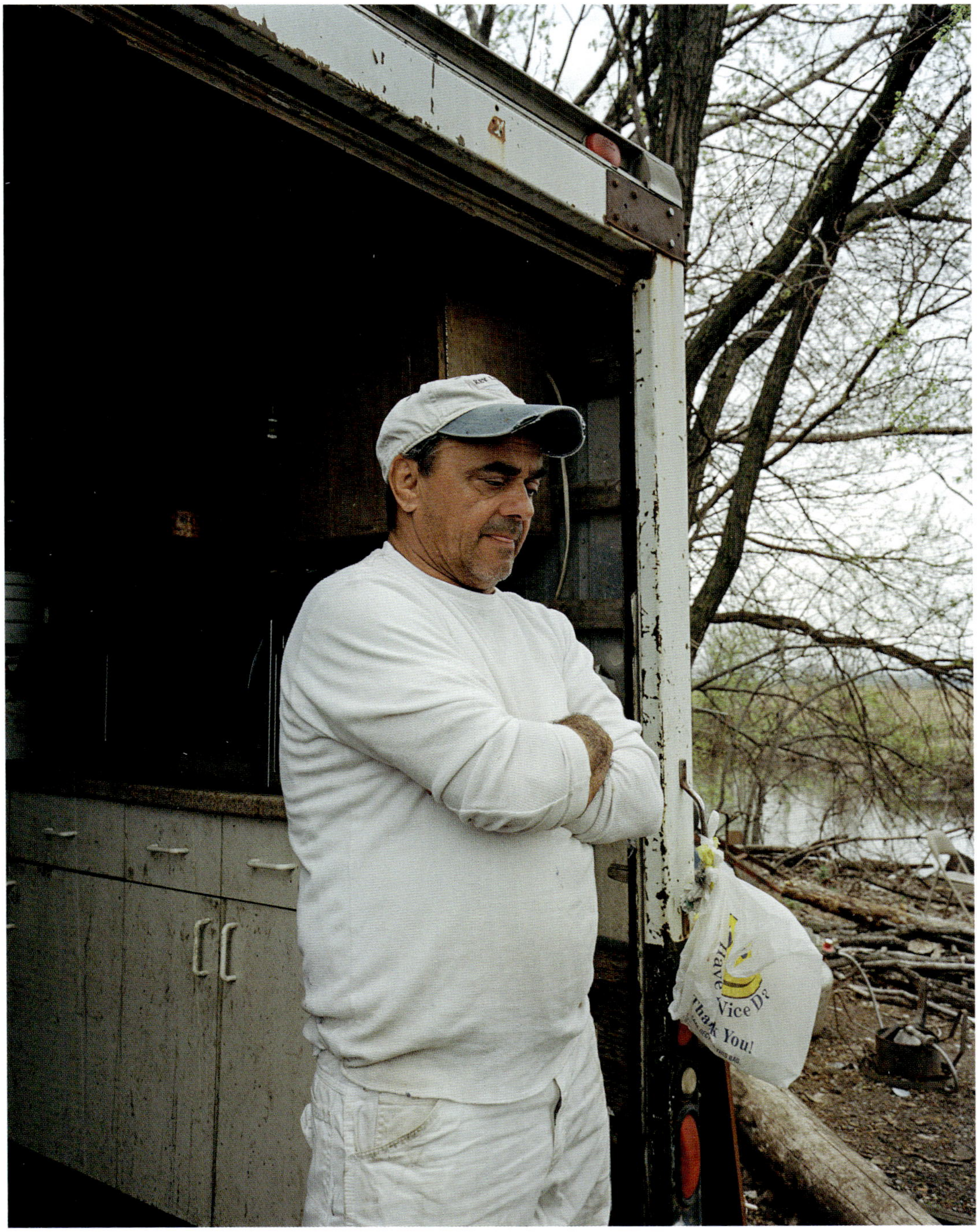
Thank You!

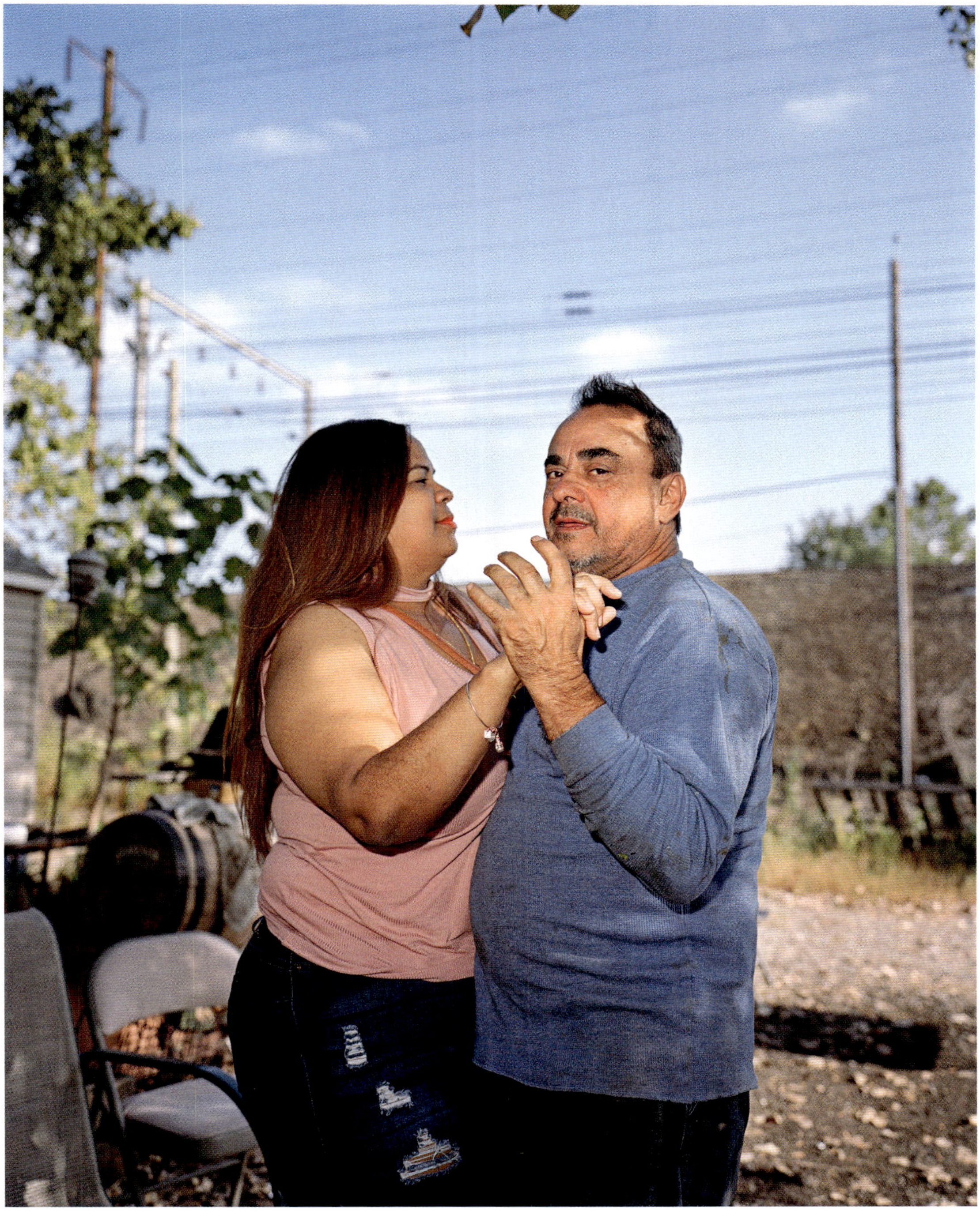

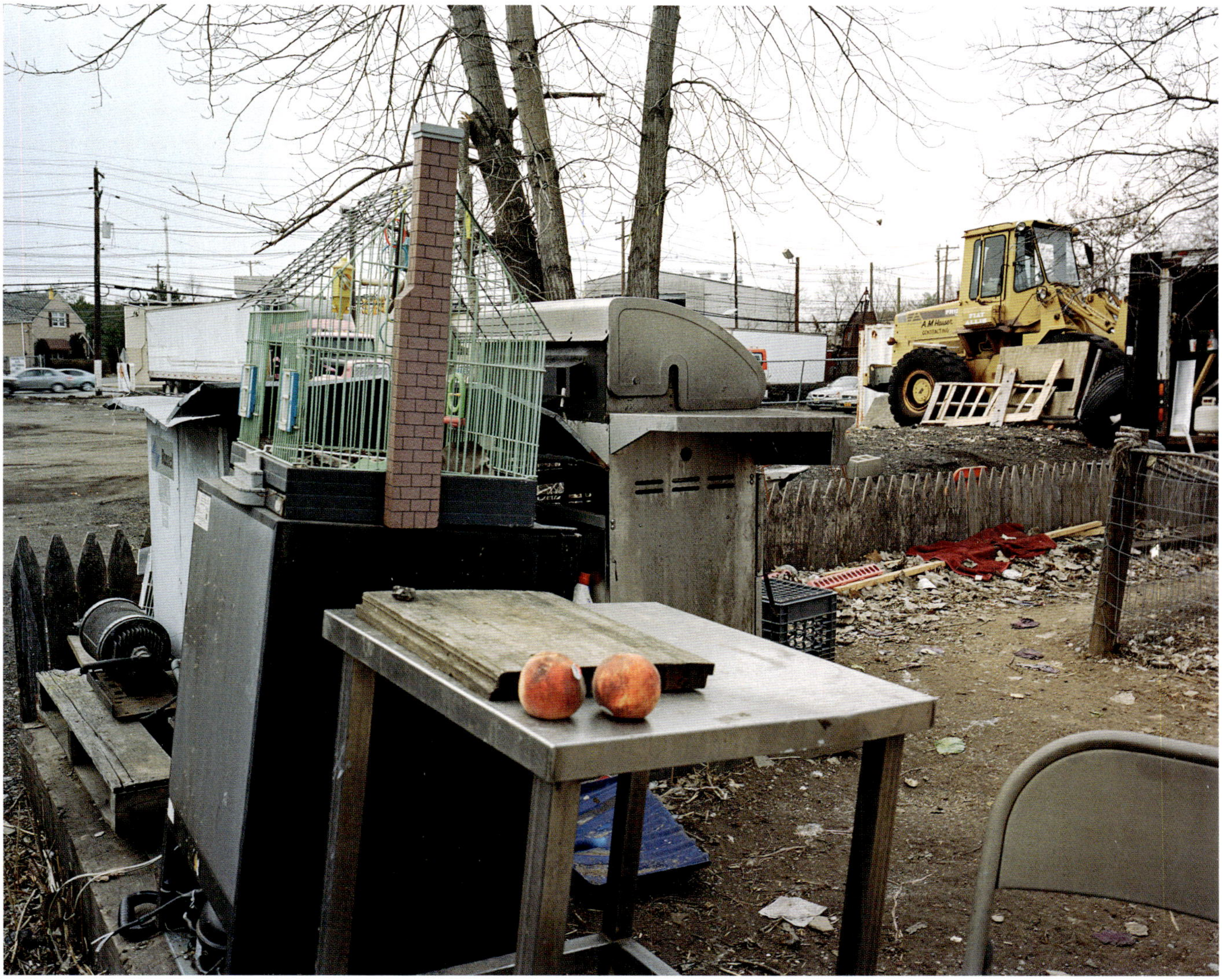

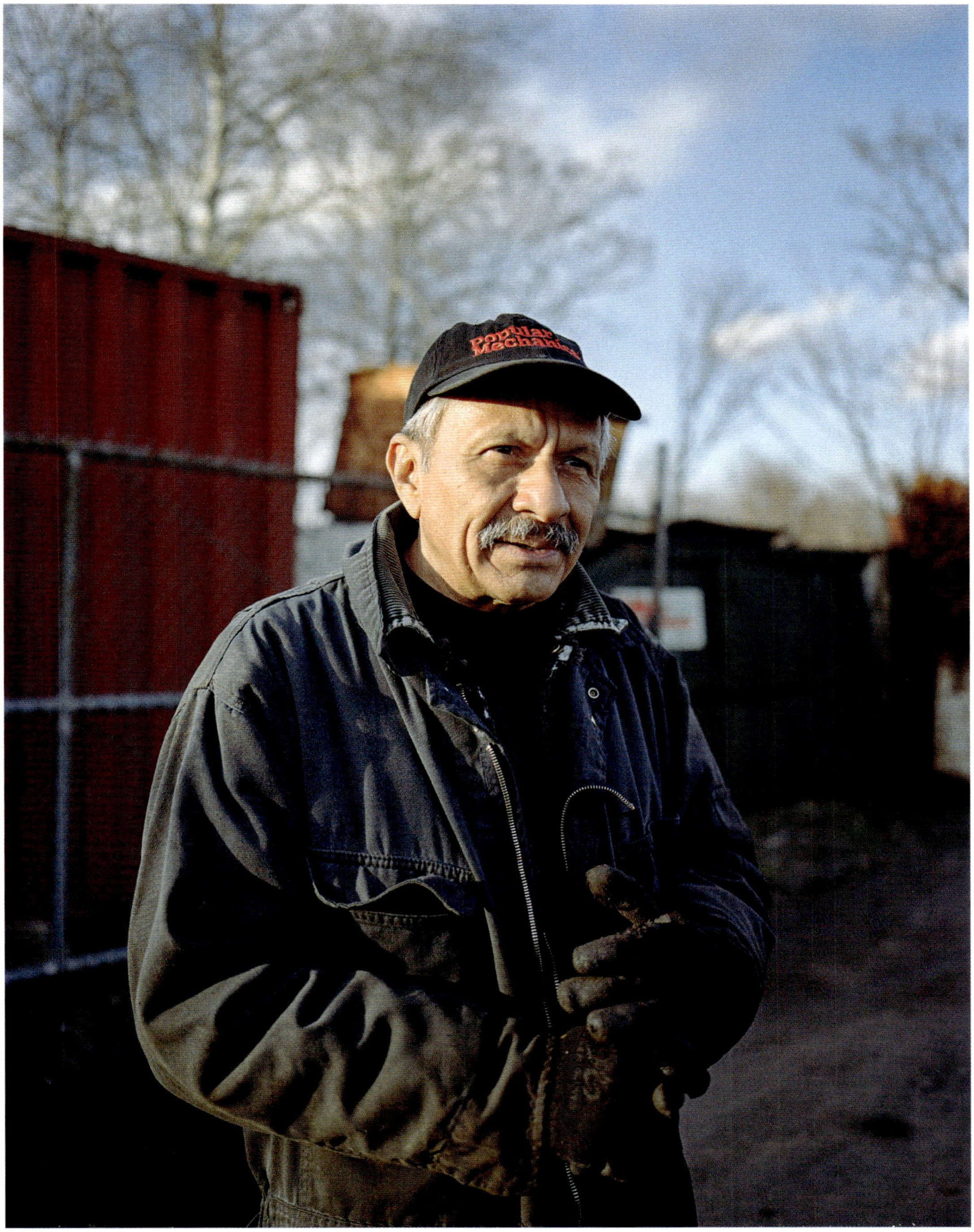
Popular
Mechanics

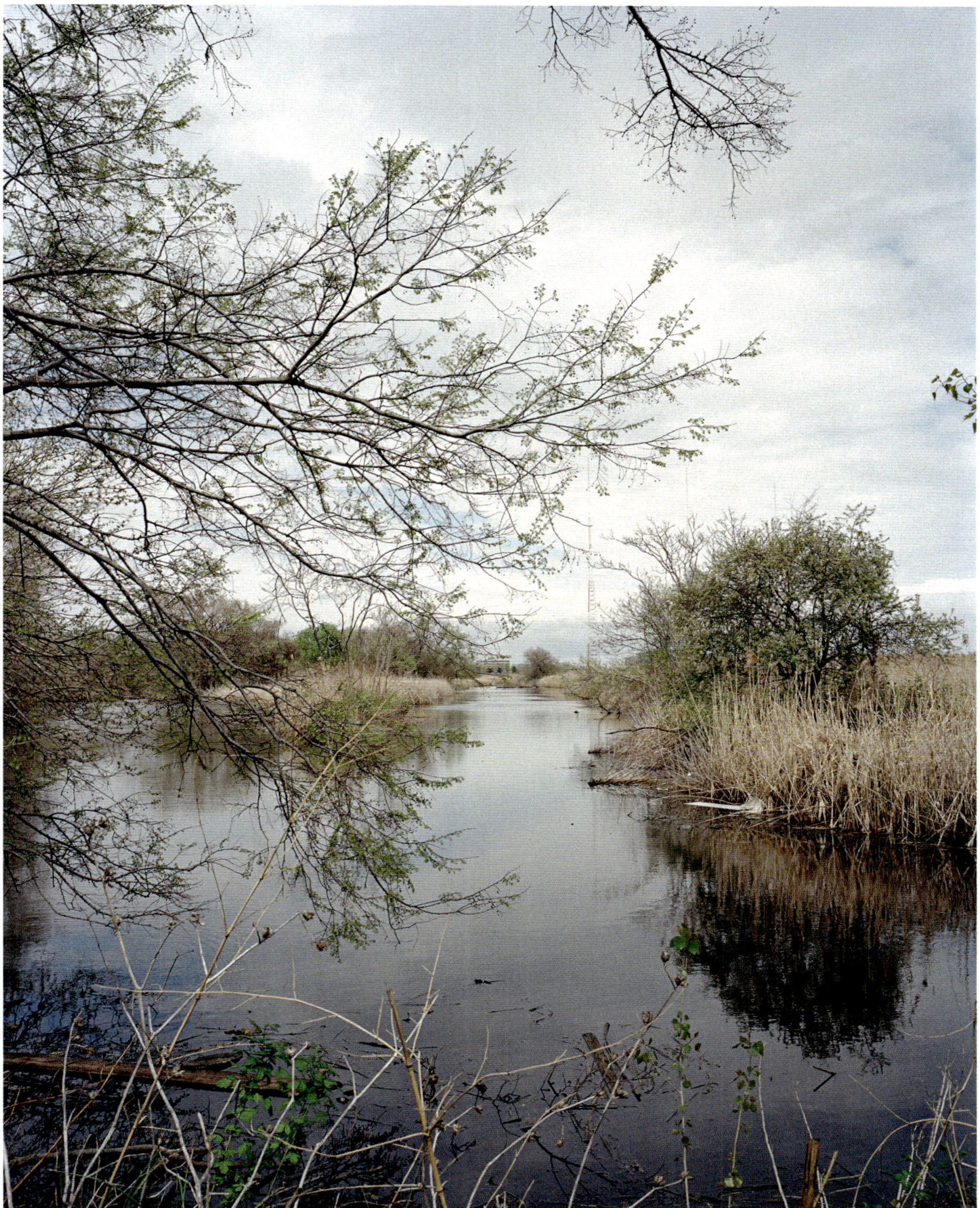

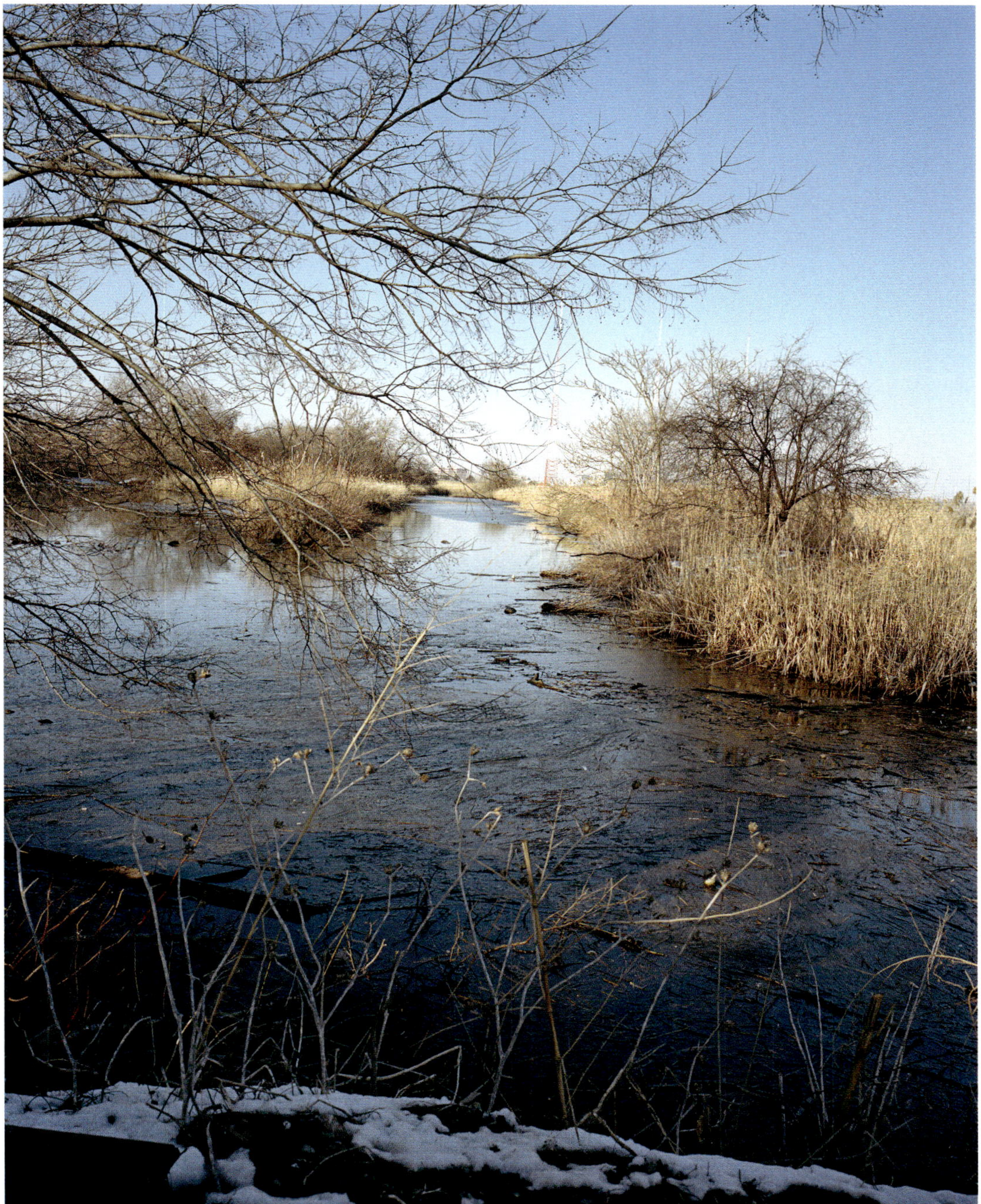

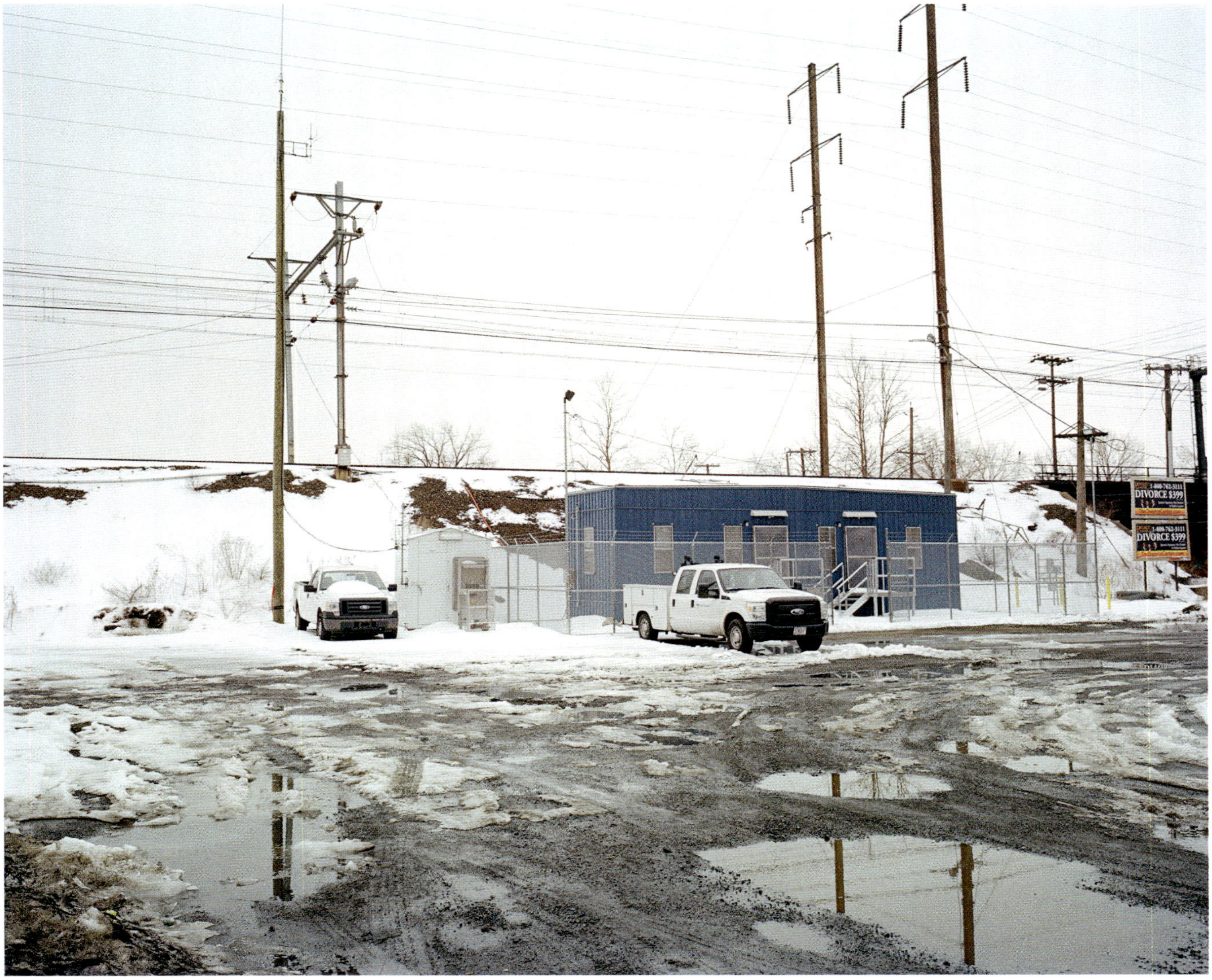
DIVORCE $399
DIVORCE $399

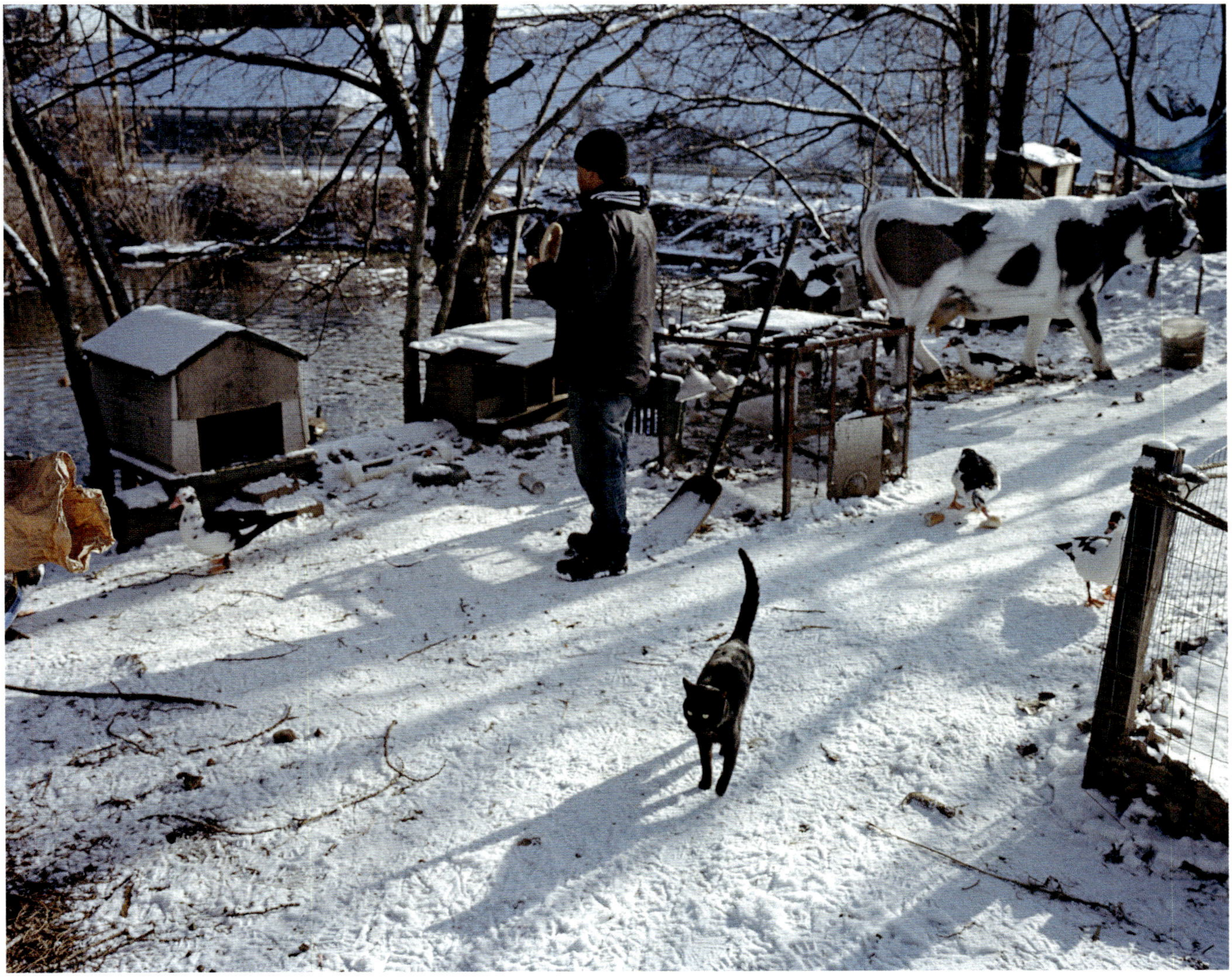

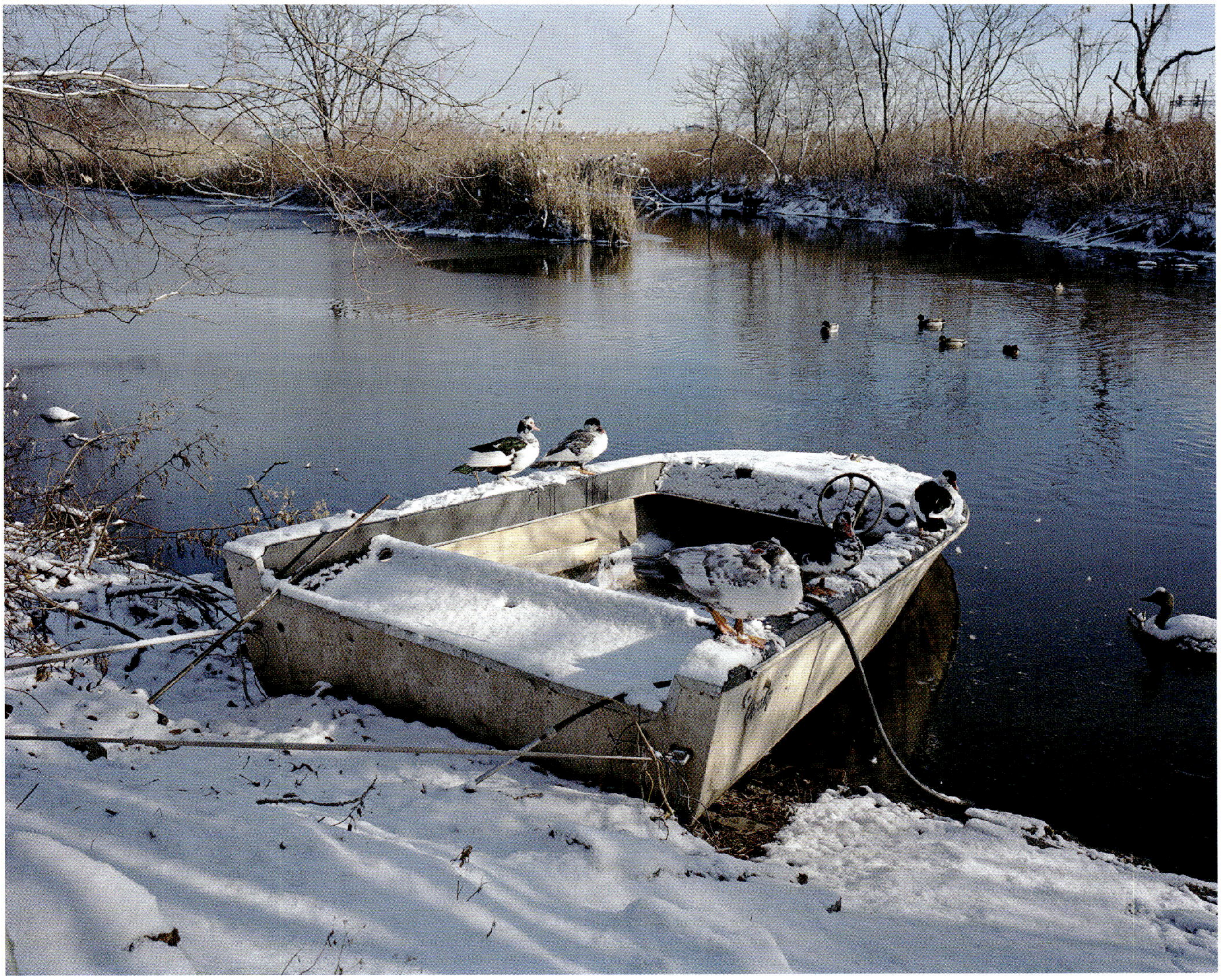

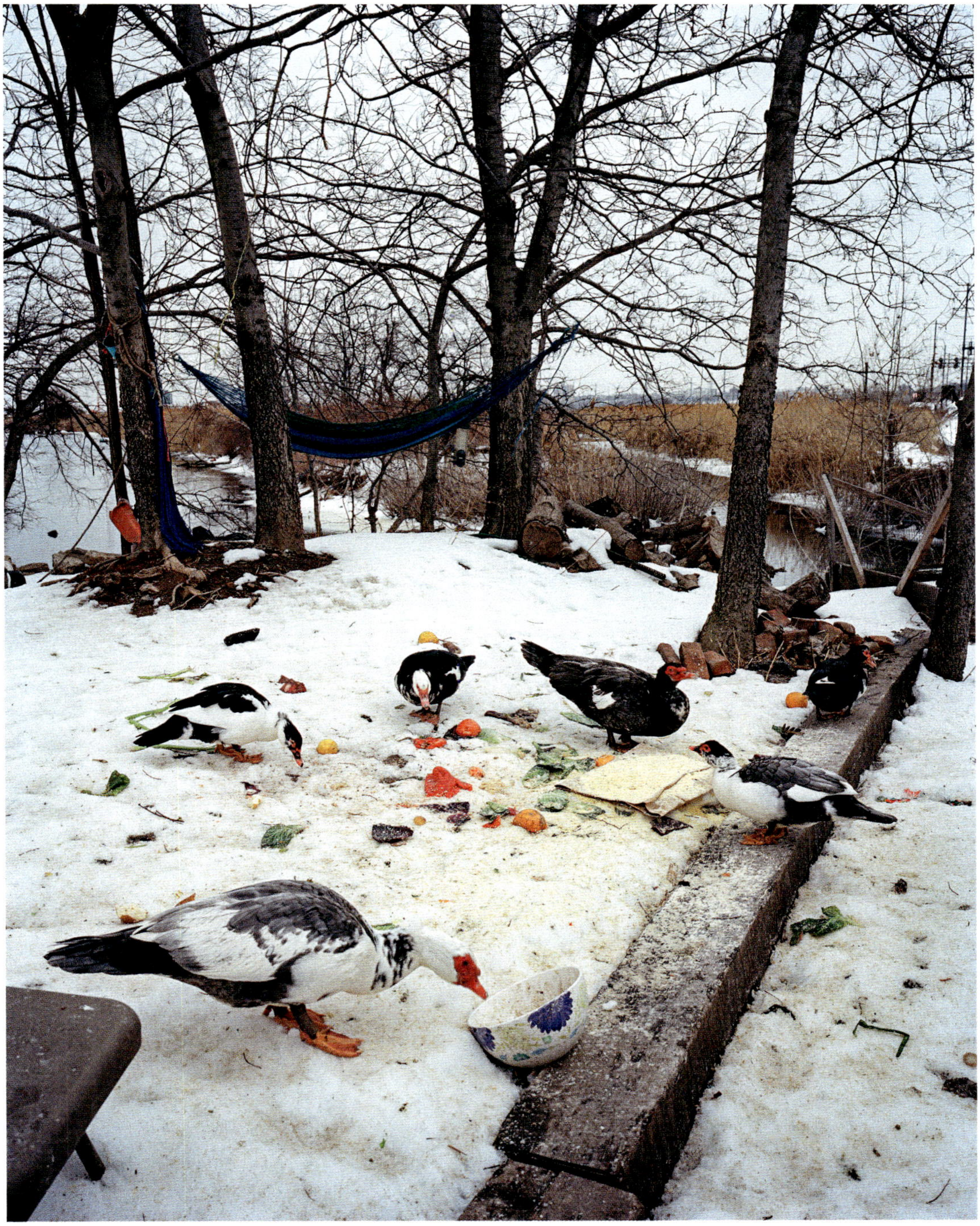

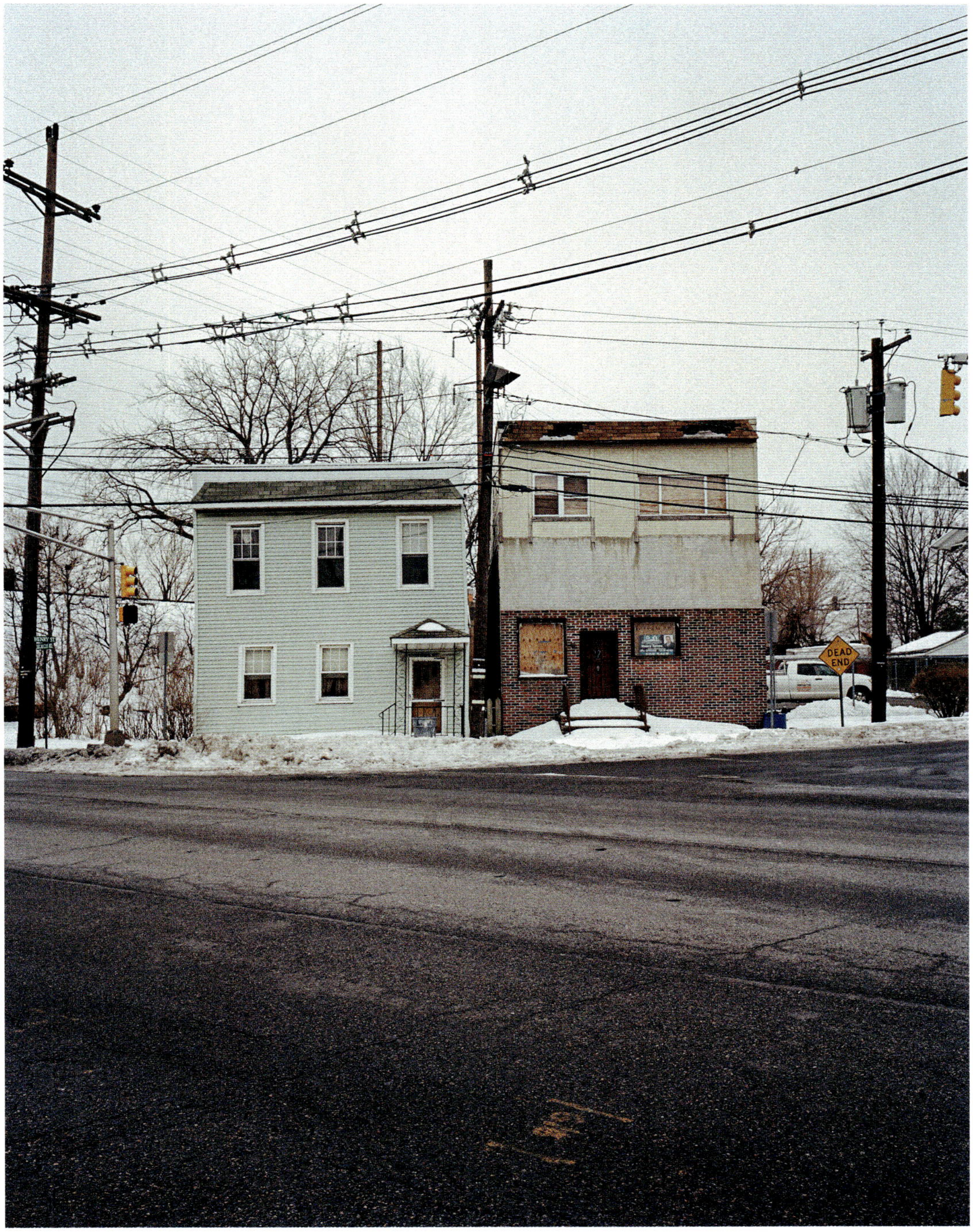
DEAD
END

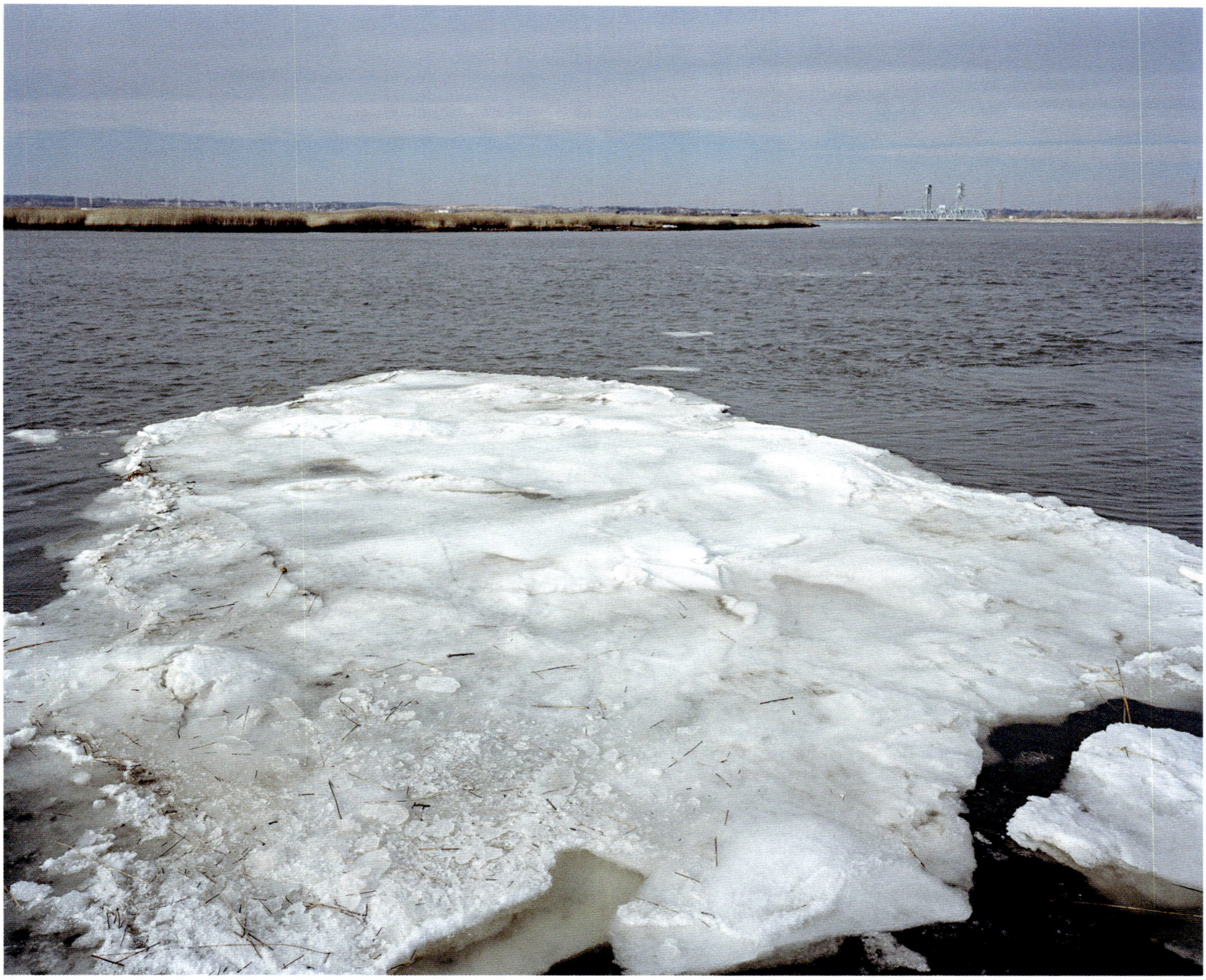

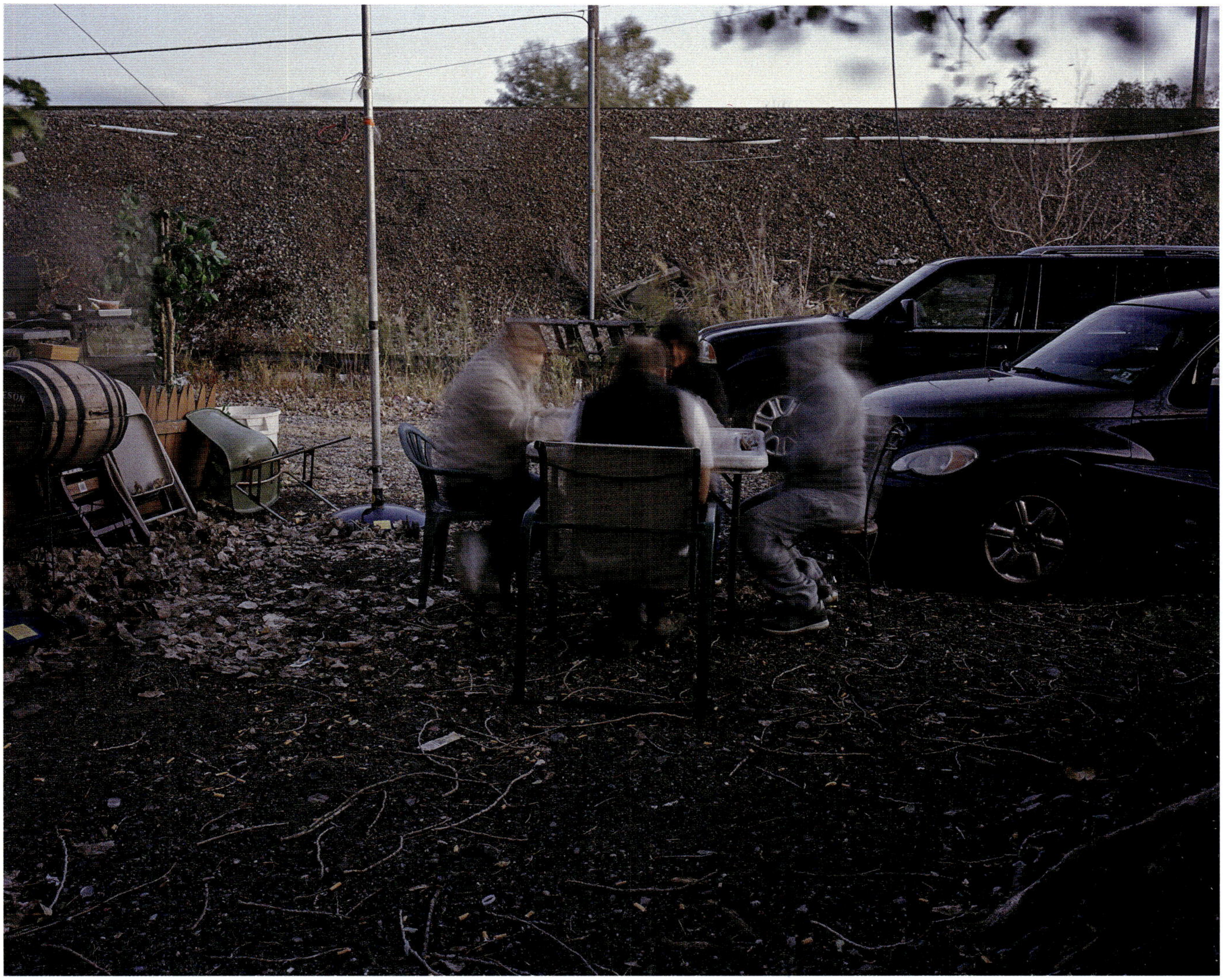

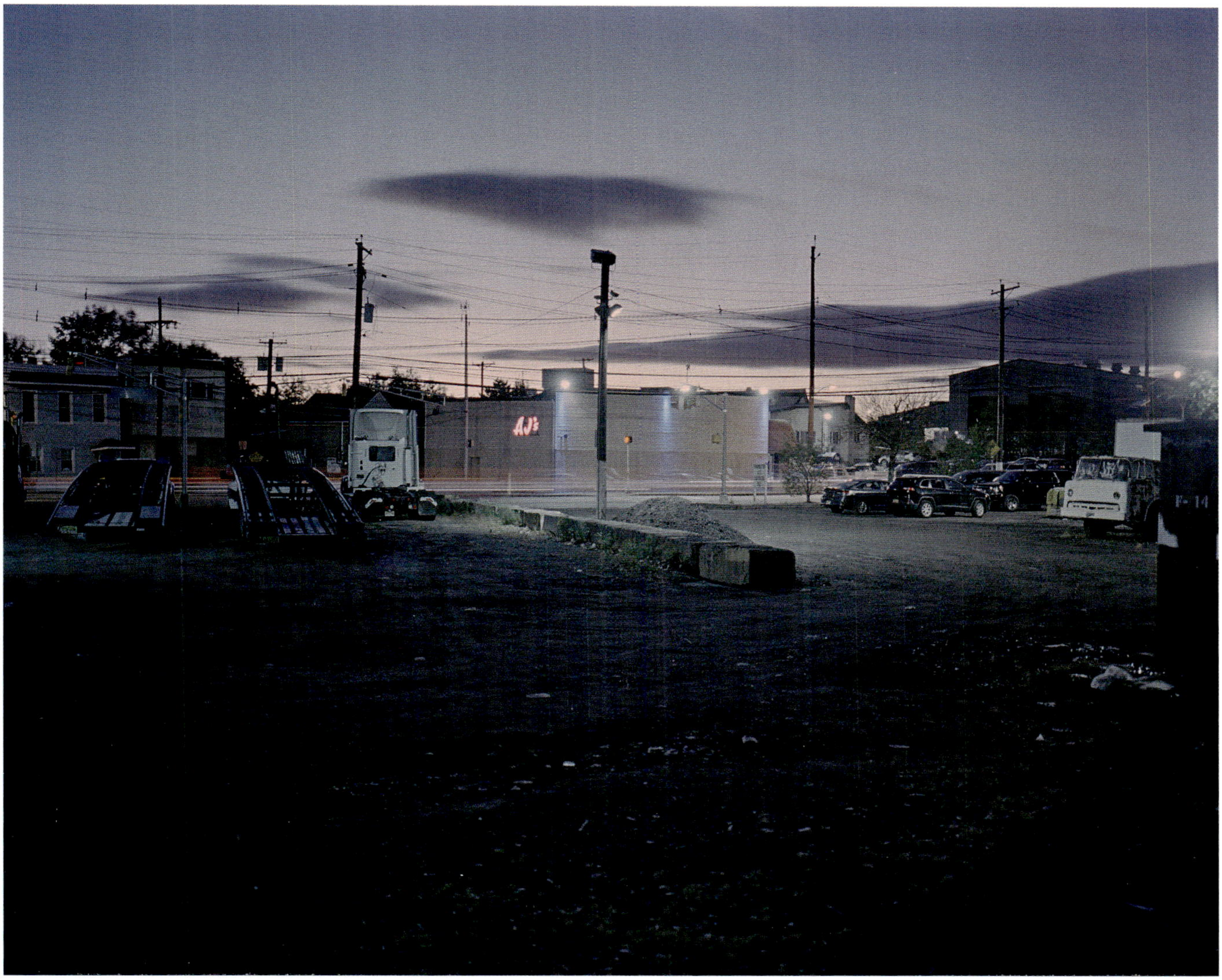
AJ's

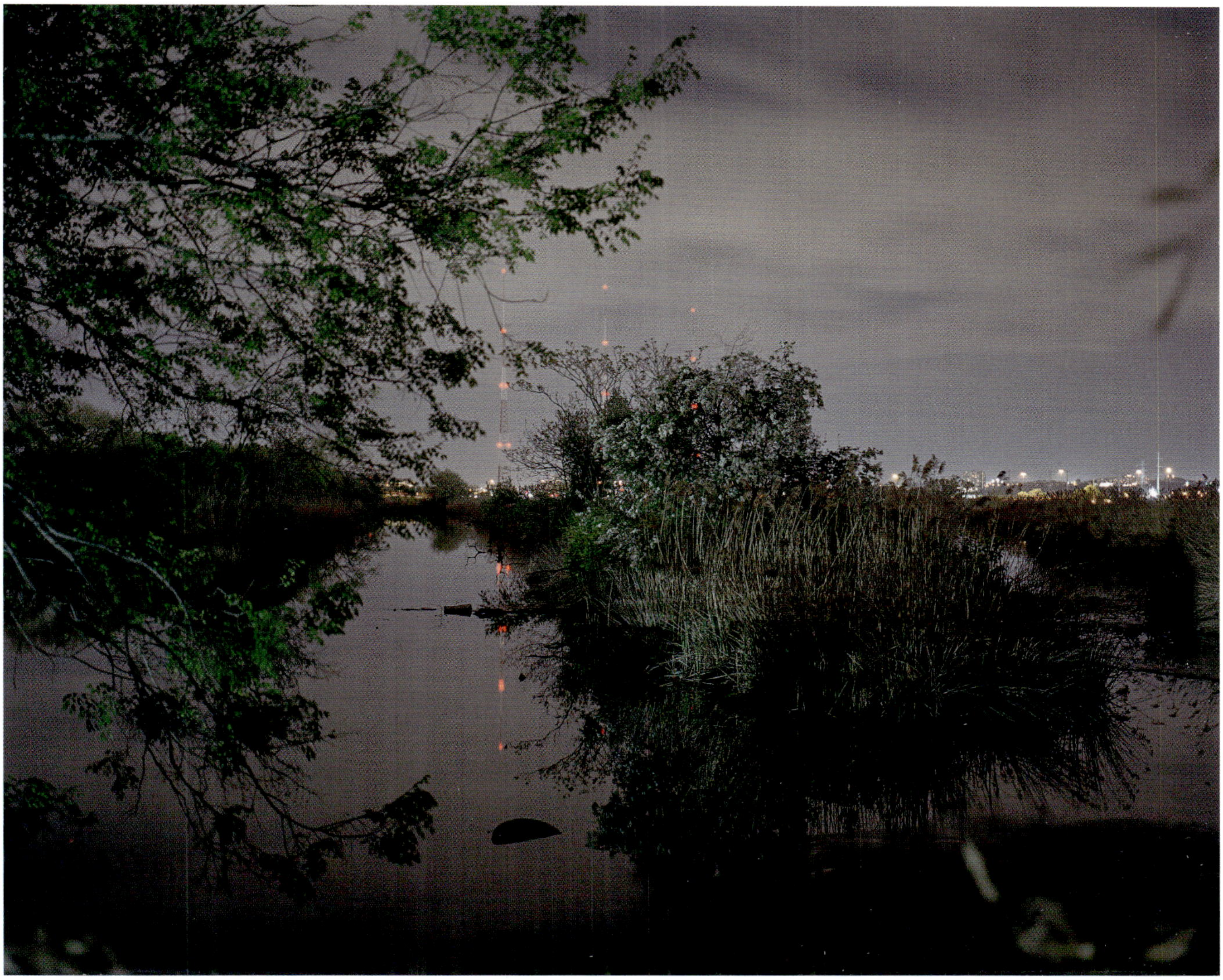

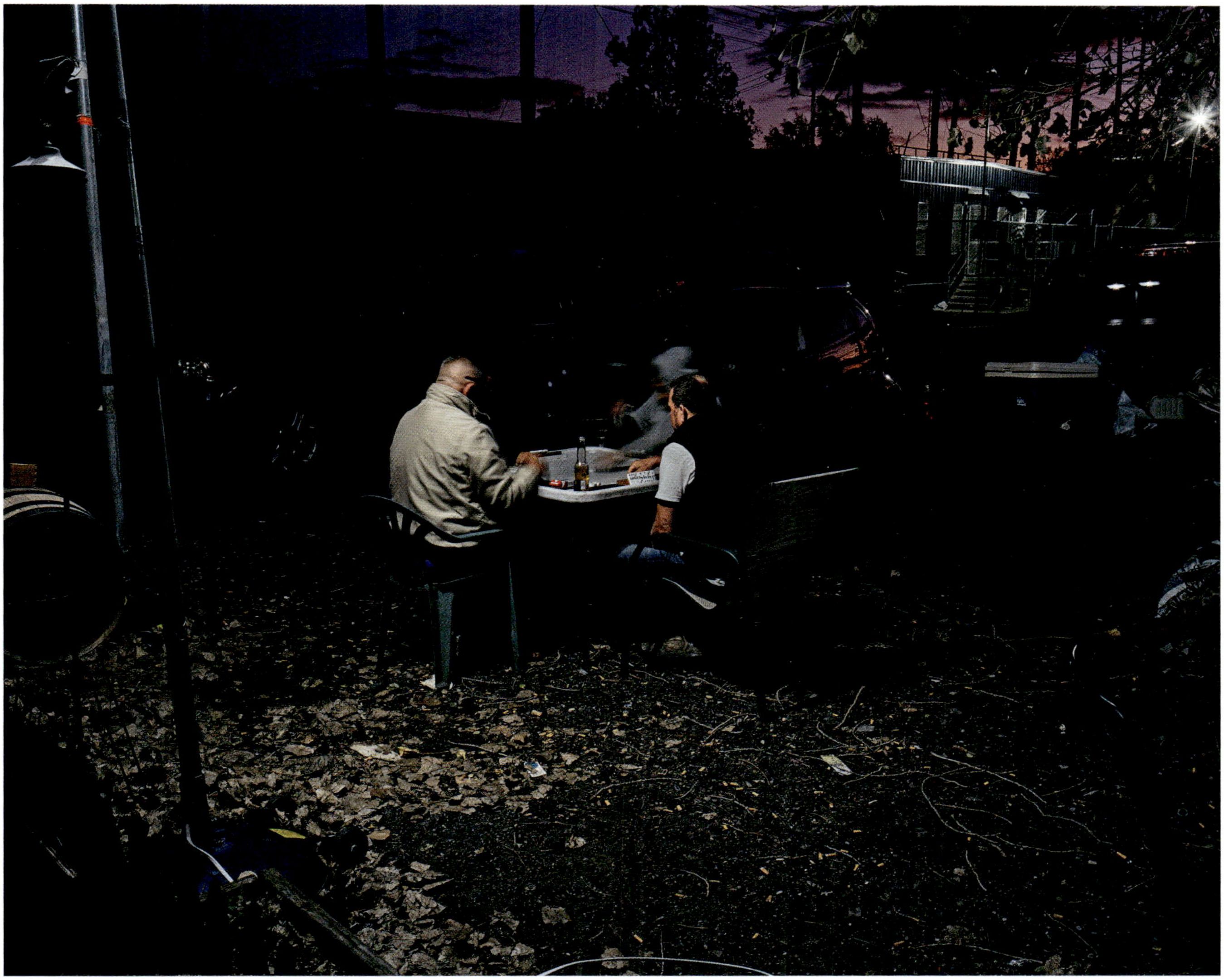

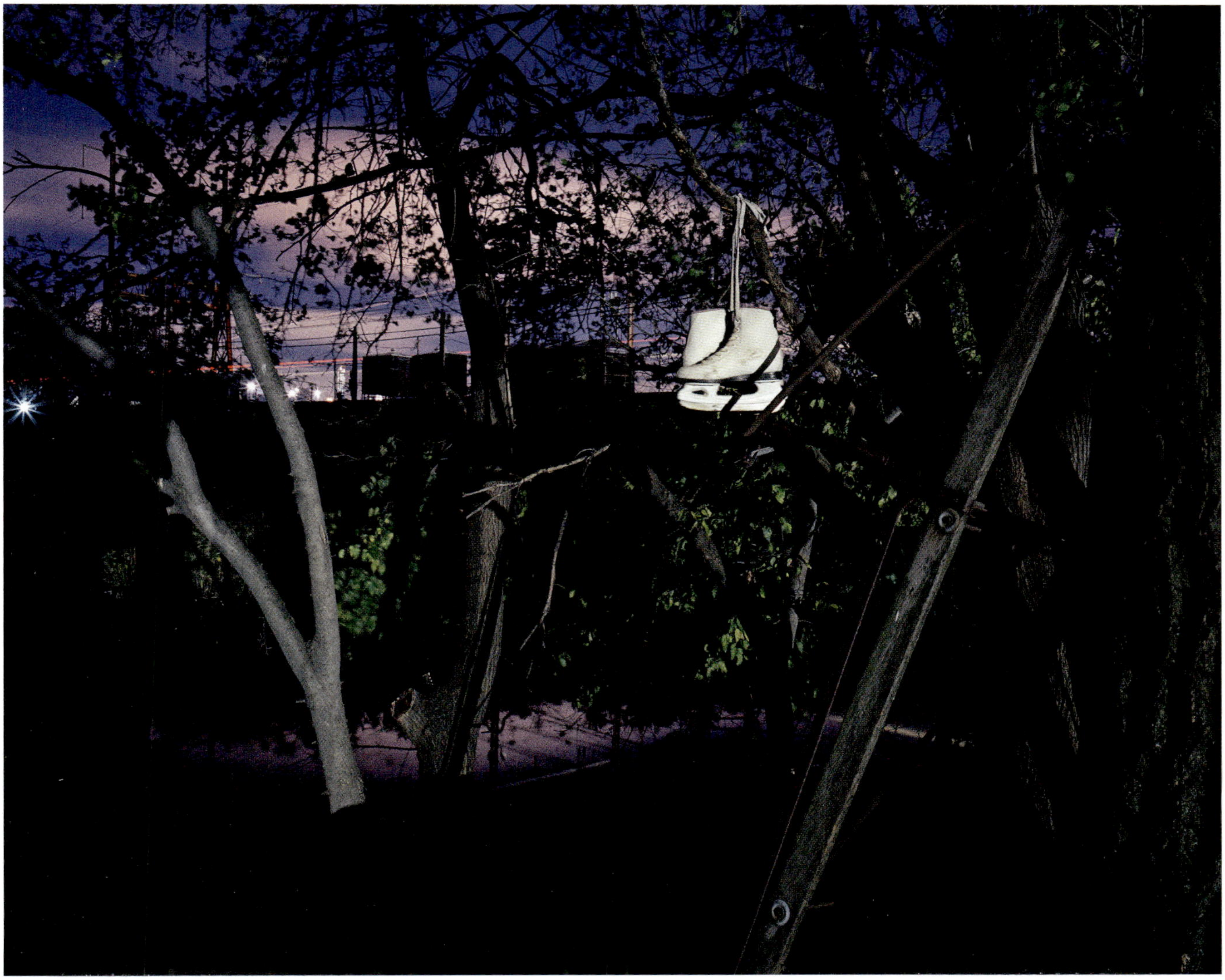

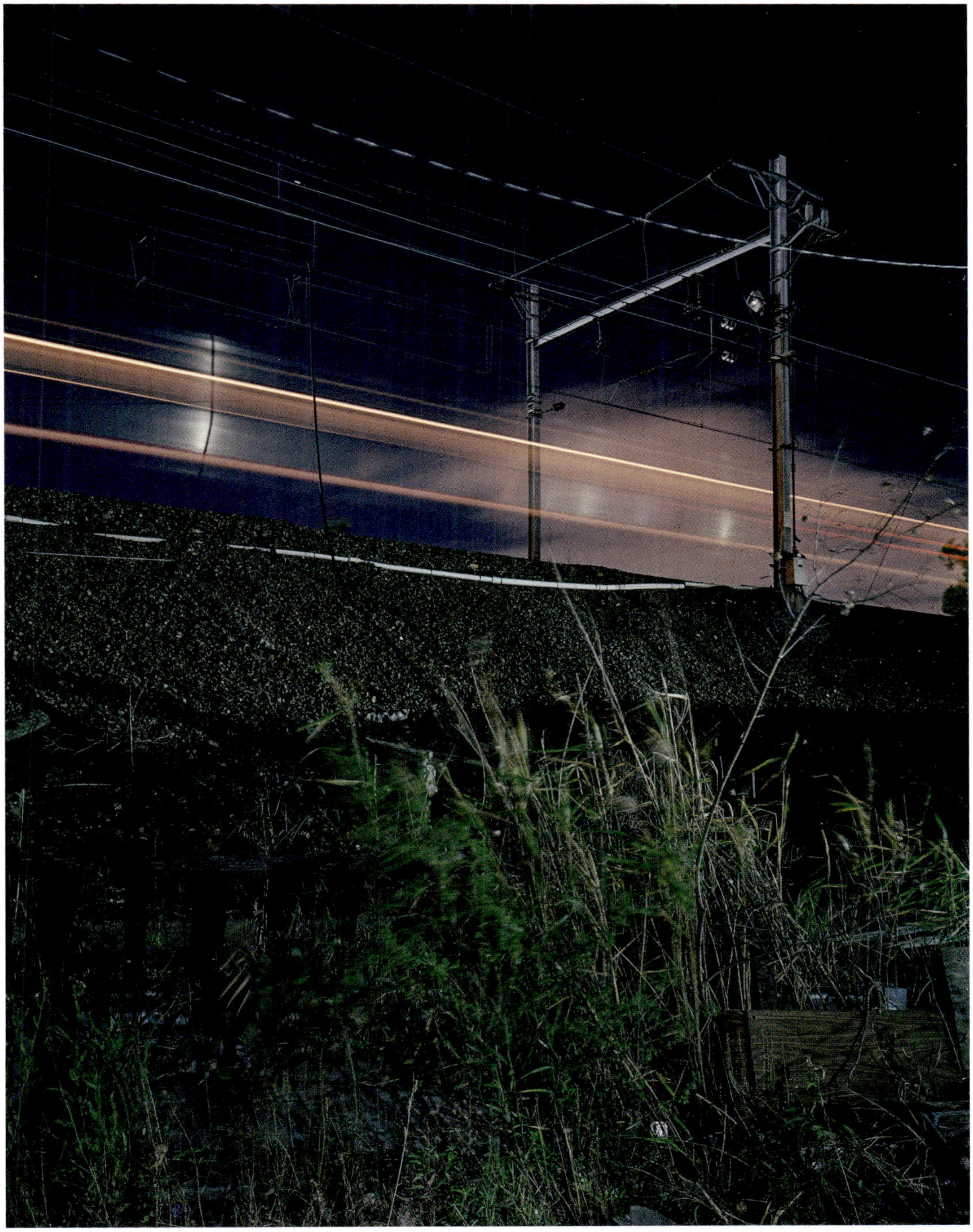

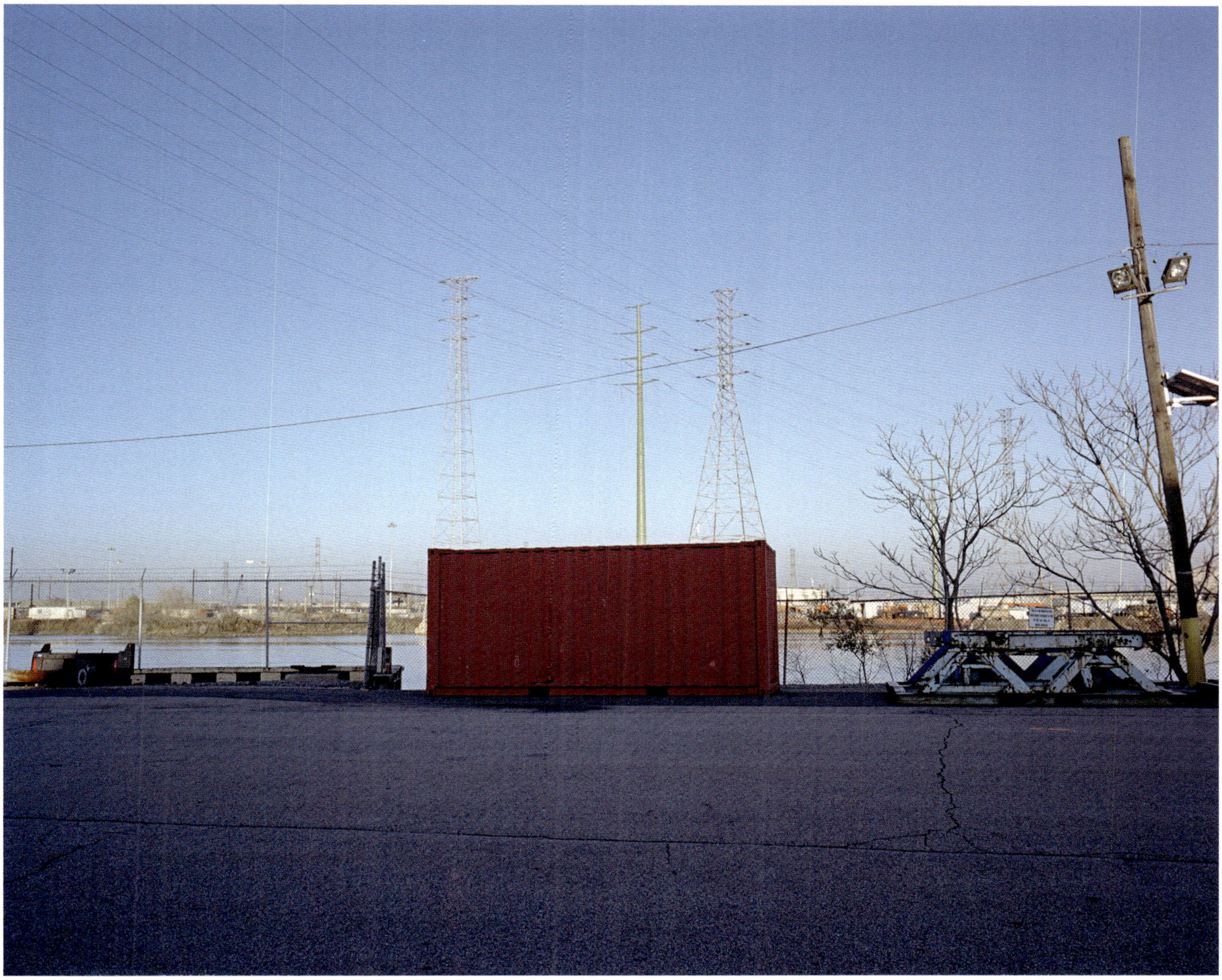

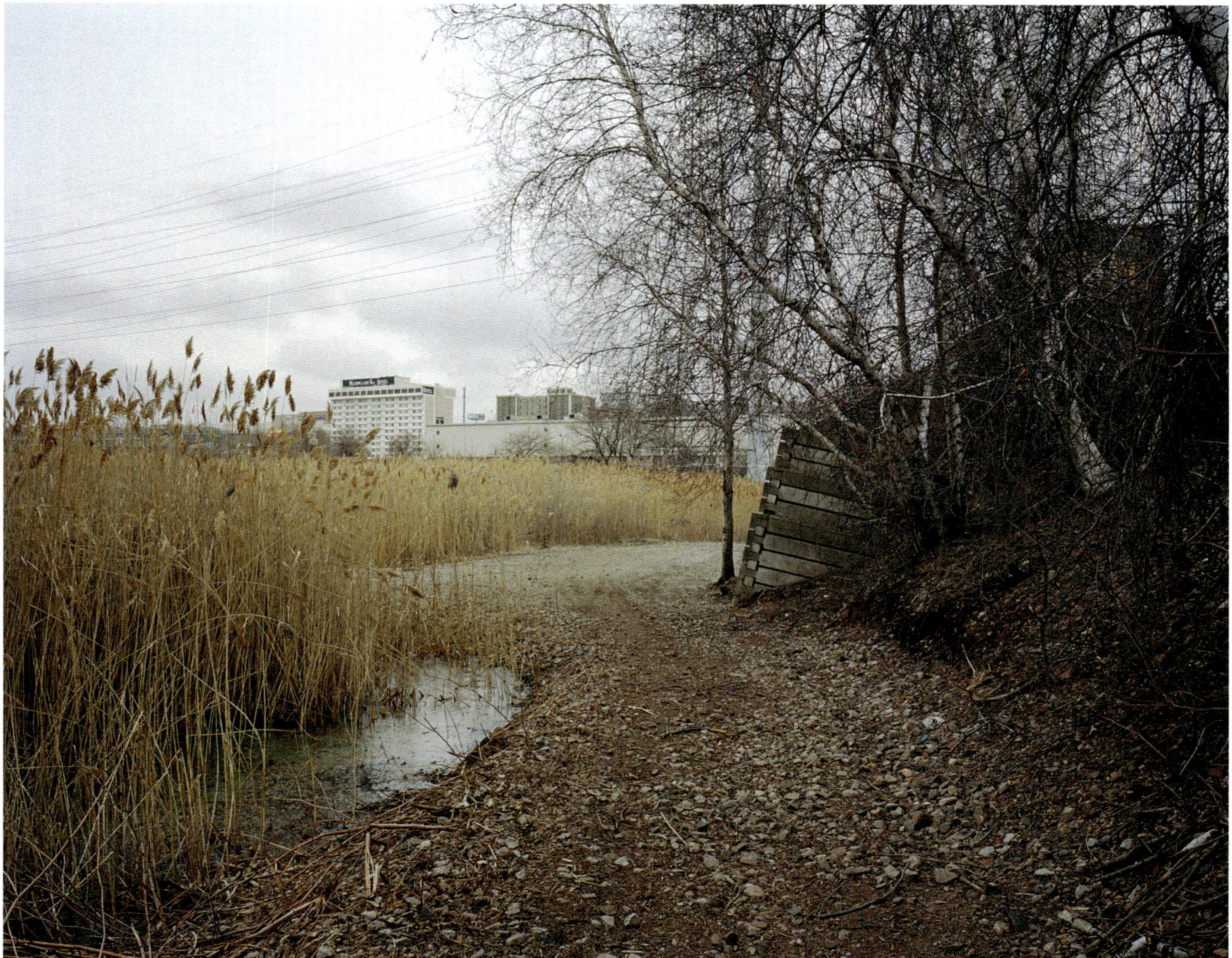

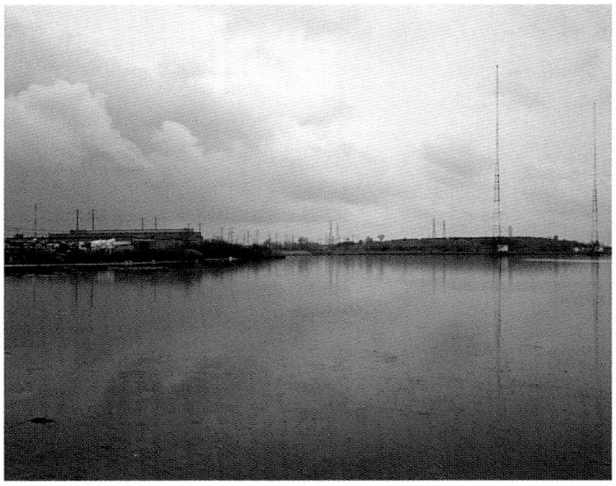
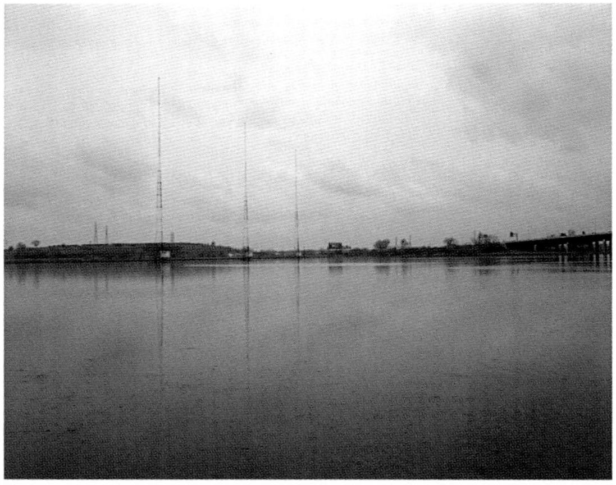
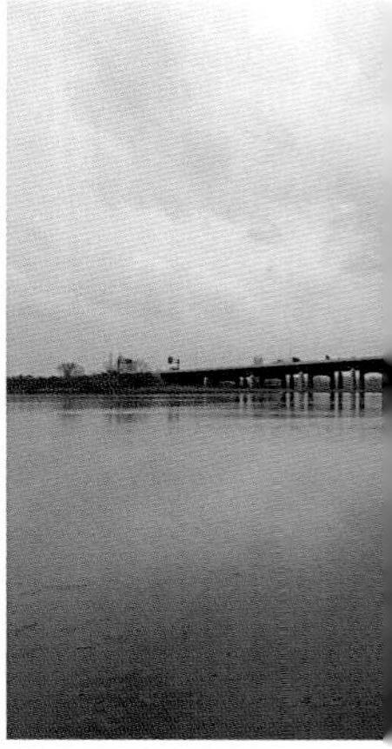

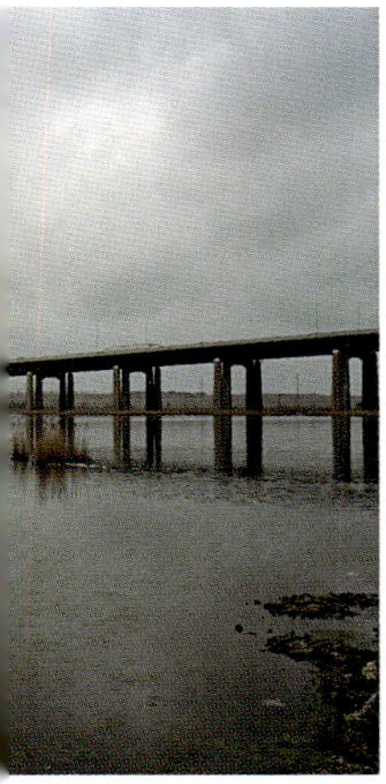

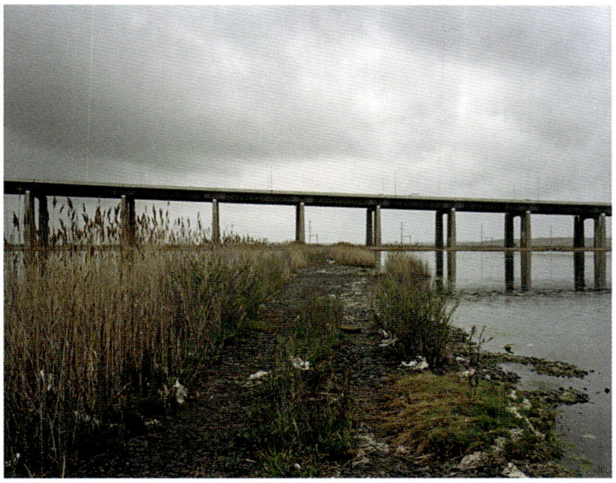

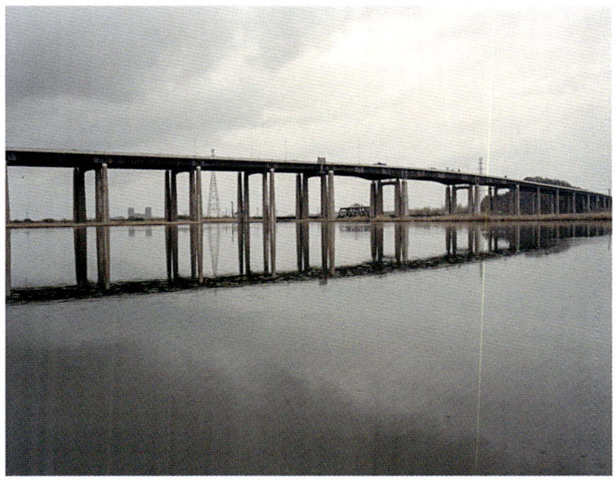

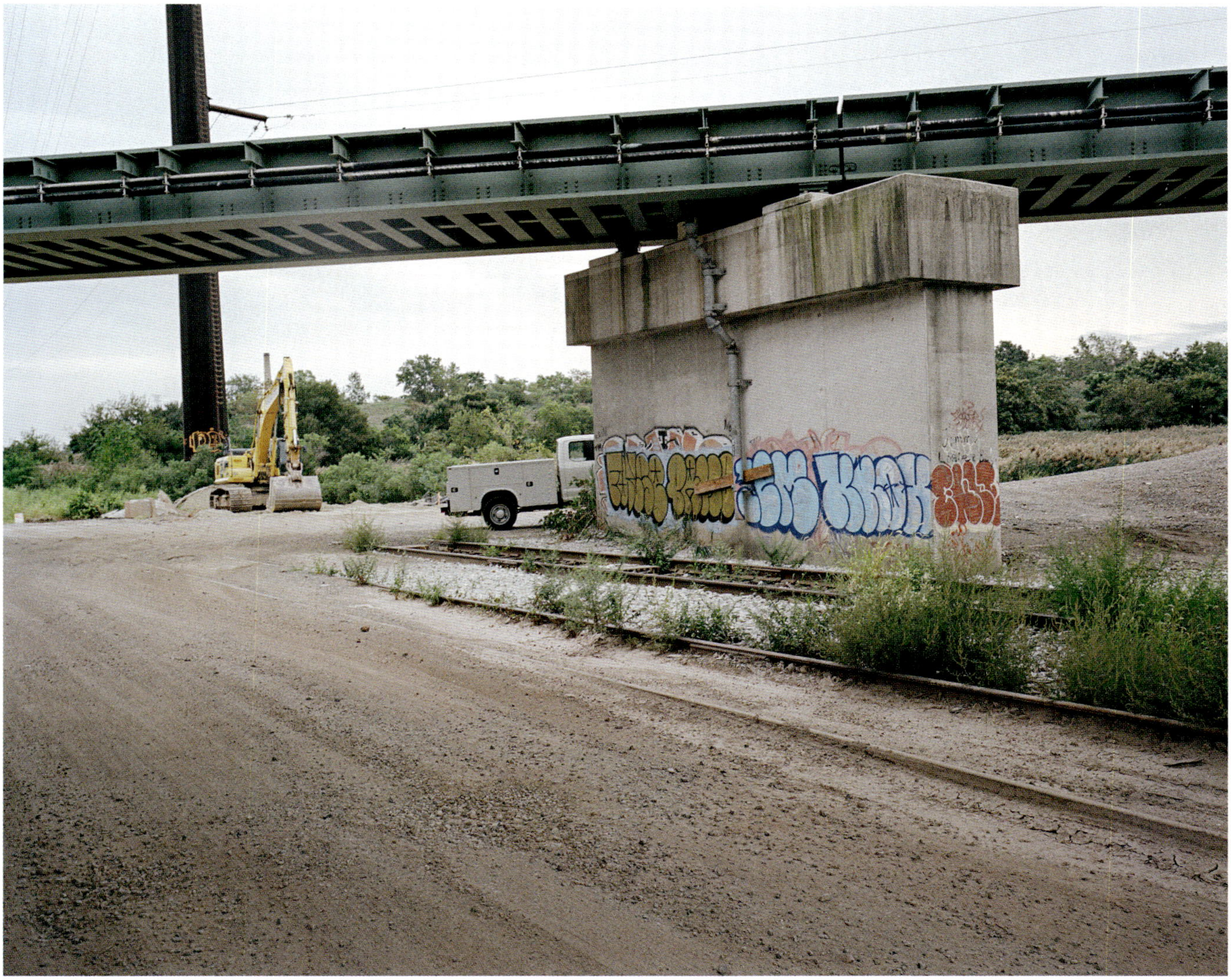

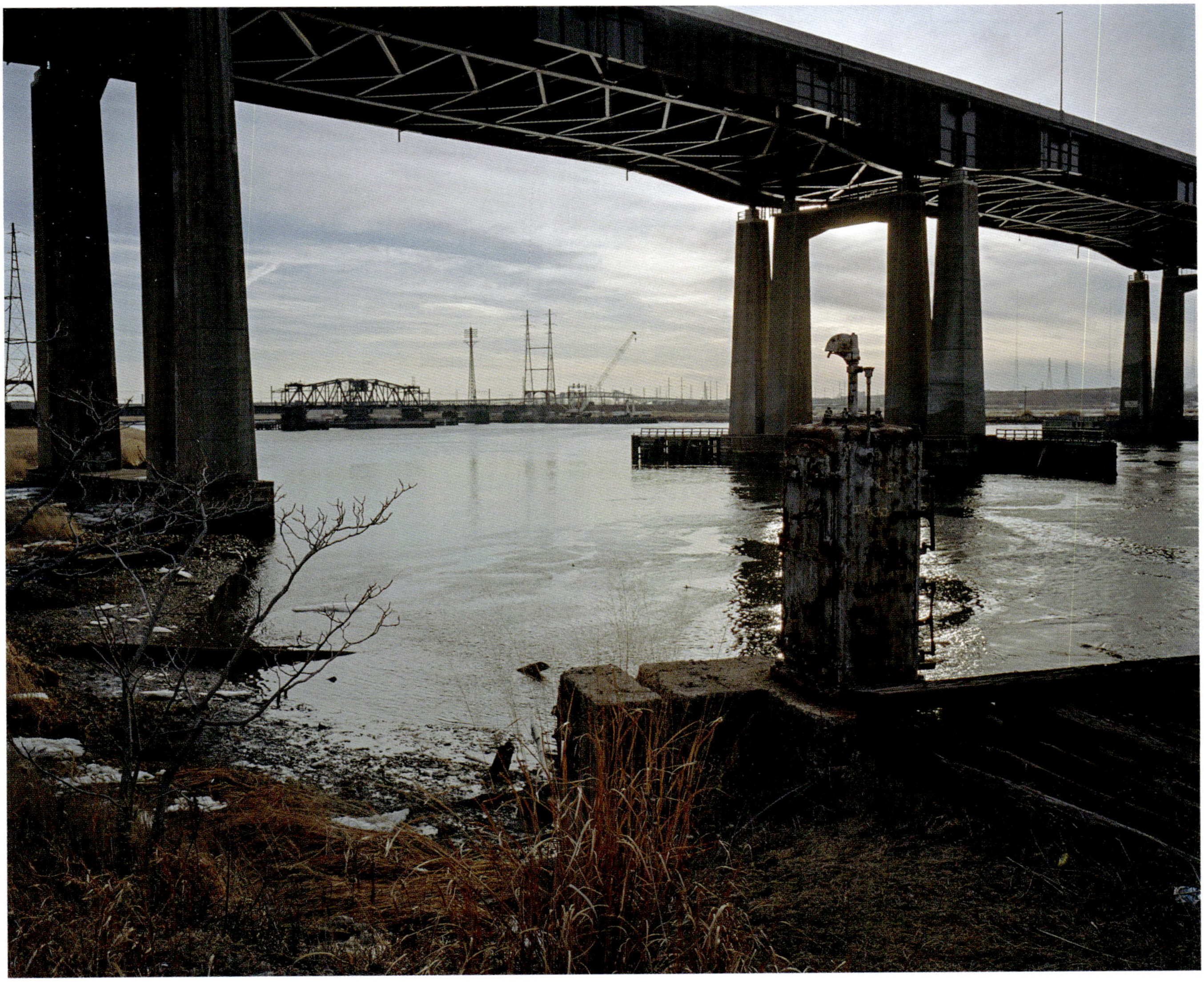

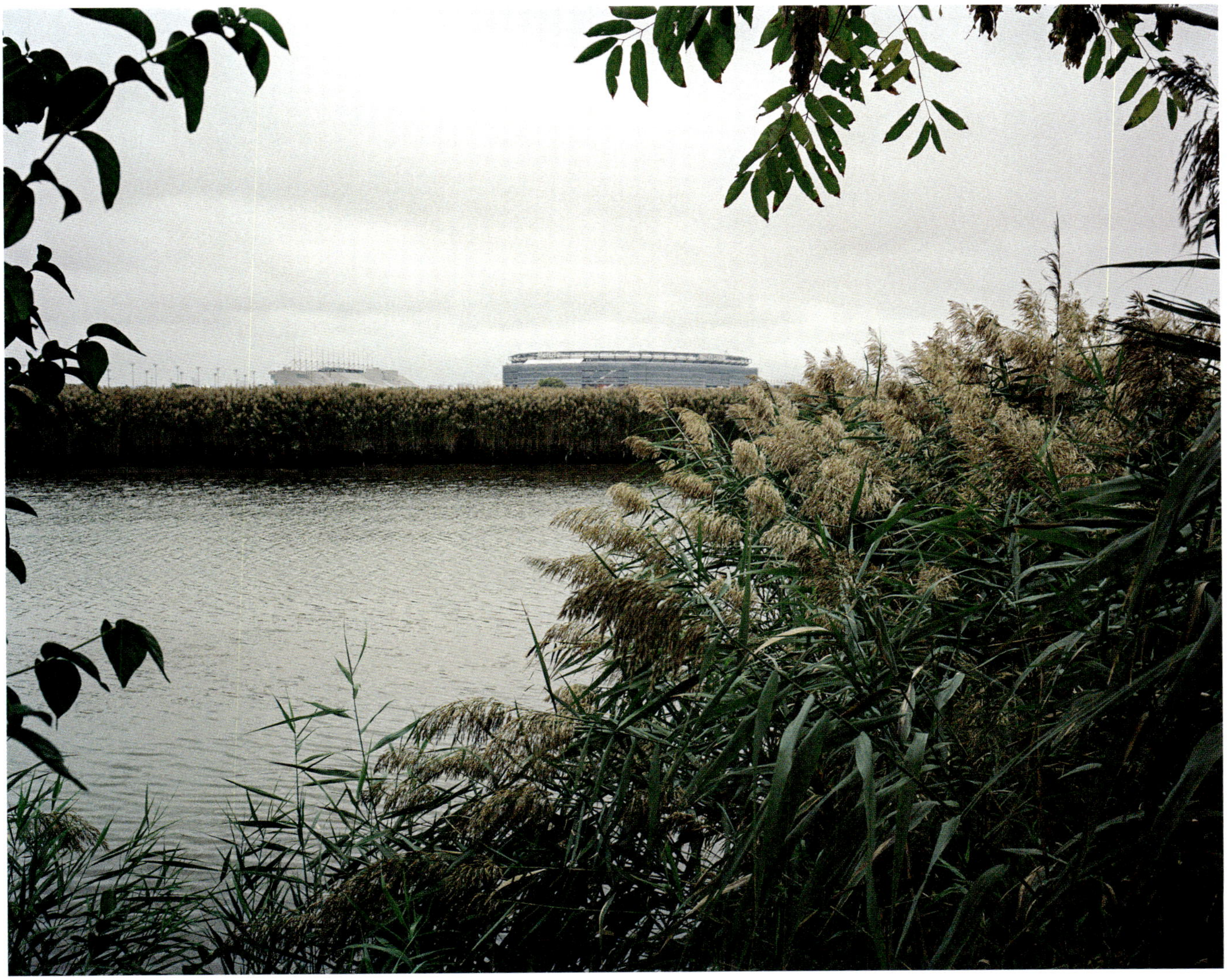

Eugene was born in Cuba. He was raised in Miami, and later made his way to New Jersey.

He told me he remembers cooking barefoot over an open fire with his grandma in Cuba, animals running all around. It's a happy memory he tells me about as he sets up a propane burner and prepares some shrimp. We are living in his memory as he tells it—cats and ducks and rabbits are all around us, there are tomatoes and corn growing in the garden, the place where we are is next to the railroad tracks but everyone here is a trucker. The dominoes table is set up and a couple of the guys are having beers, waiting for Eugene and the other players.

"You want a beer," Eugene takes a cold Corona out of the cooler in the box truck kitchen for me. "I'm the most generous man in the world." He looks at me: "You don't believe me yet, but you'll see, I am the most generous man in the world." He continues preparing the meal as more cars start to pull up in the gravel lot next door.

The cars could be more guys coming for dominoes and food, sometimes it's someone heading to AJ's or an Amtrak worker, but usually the sound of tires crunching on gravel means more beers. A train whooshes by and in the echo of its path there is a brief stillness, a silence only noticed by the geese bobbing in the marshy waters of Penhorn Creek. A red-winged blackbird sings, and Eugene smiles at the birdseed he hung from the trees: "they love it here."

Nicholas Pollack
Brooklyn, NY, 2020

Here find *meadow* remarked, recorded, made apparent, reshaped, perhaps scythed, as meadows are—or were. Here find *marsh* too.

Nursery rhyme instructs. *The sheep's in the meadow* signals something awry. Meadow pastures neither horse nor cow, and certainly not grass-cropping, grass-killing sheep. Livestock graze in pastures, not meadows. In meadows grows grass, grass for mowing, the grass that morphs into hay, wintertime fodder for livestock snugged in barns.

Meadow proves hoary. Deep-rooted in obscure pre-Old Teutonic speech, *mædwâ* became the Old English *mǽdwe* and in Old Frisian *mêde*. In Middle High German, it became *matte*. The core ancient root is *mē*, to mow, to cut grass: the term is as old as the keeping of livestock through cold, snowy winters. Its sister term, the feminine Old English *mǽd*, also denoted a field kept mowed (and in spring covered with bees), but gradually disappeared, lingering in nineteenth-century poetry and stolid still in English place names, especially Agatha Christie's *St. Mary Mead*. But the name of a drink made of fermented honey is rooted perhaps in a Sanskrit word designating sweetness: it became the Old Irish *medd,* and the modern Welsh *medd* and English *mead*. Extant since 969 in written English, *meadow* flourished in all sorts of spellings, *meddoe* being one common variant, and kept its significance and meaning as it slowly effaced its sister term. Economically, geographically, and socially important, the term continuously connoted the vital necessity of overwintering livestock.

In places critical in the breeding of cows and horses—say the Frisian region of The Netherlands, Herefordshire in England, and the Jersey Channel Islands—the term shimmers in significance. Premium-quality hay feeds pure-bred breeding stock, improves herd quality, and focuses attention on meadows, the ground itself of deep-cold livestock survival.

Colonists at first used *meadow* as they had in England. But soon its meaning evolved to indicate damp, moist, or wet land, land too muddy to plow. In his 1859 *Dictionary of the English Language,* Joseph E. Worcester—the great and now-forgotten rival of Noah Webster—noted that New Englanders had long distinguished between English grass grown on upland soil and *meadow grass* or *meadow hay*, more coarse than the invasive grass, soon called *English grass* (still the grass of front lawns), born of seeds in hay brought across the Atlantic as shipboard livestock fodder. In his 1859 *Dictionary of Americanisms*, New Yorker John Russell Bartlett understood the usage as national: "in the United States often applied to mowing lands which are marshy or too wet to be ploughed, and producing a coarse kind of hay, which is called *meadow* hay."

But always *meadow* clashed with *marsh*. It clashes here. *Marsh* is hoary too, but wet, usually but not always scented with salt, the salt of the sea, in Old Teutonic *mari*, designating the sea or sprawling fresh water like Lake Windermere. In Old English it was *męrsc*, naming land at the edges of *meres*, routinely flooded, often in winter, then in Middle Dutch, *mersche*, then in a variety of modern English variants, often dialect synonyms (some brought across the Channel by Netherlanders hired to drain immense watery tracts in Norfolk and Suffolk), *mersche*, *marsch*, and *march*, and finally (so far) *marsh* (the last pronounced in multiple ways, *mash* once common between Manhattan and Philadelphia). While *medder* or *meddah* remained a common pronunciation of *meadow* north of New York City, *mash* connoted more than its regional pronunciation to the south might seem to indicate. The *Dictionary of American Regional English* notes that by 1894 in New Jersey, *marsh* and *meadow* sometimes worked as synonyms, *meadow* denoting "a salty marshy tract used for grazing and 'shingling,'" something vexingly important in the images. Livestock almost never graze in meadows. Cows and horses wandering into marshes, especially salt marshes washed by the tides, in the *matted* (a living word rooted in the Middle

High German root of *meadow*) grassy ground, they often flounder, break legs, and sometimes drown. But as late as 1945, the *DARE* notes some New Jersey locals pronouncing *meadow* as *medder* when mourning the loss of the haying business in the long-cleared wetland remarked in the pages which follow here.

Dutch colonists felled the white-cedar trees that grew in the wet soil (the cedar indicating the fresh-water nature of the soil), cut them into short chunks, then split them into roofing shingles. As they had at home, they struggled to drain the land, channeling the Hackensack and other fresh and tidal flows in what became a half-successful effort that created from forest a vast landscape of light. The land remained too wet to plow, but was soon productive of good hay, easily scythed and economically barged to Manhattan, an enterprise that began to fail only with the proliferation of automobiles. As haying collapsed, so did the maintenance of ditches, canals, and sluicegates, and the meadows became marge, edgy, puddled, rail-stitched, seen-and-not-seen by commuters, but mostly unvisited, marginal, dumping ground, wasteland. Tidal surges and heavy rains flooded and still flood the entire region to which an odd term now sticks, because the landscape of light lives.

Meadowlands.

Implicit and achingly echoing in the term, a plural sense still pulses. Lands. Not a continuum, but an archipelago of places, all riven by water, sometimes marsh, sometimes something else, something beyond *meadow* and *marsh*, something beyond language.

Something for which photography exists.

John R. Stilgoe
Harvard University

These photos capture not just a place, but the mood of that place—and in so doing they remind us to constantly broaden our sense of what constitutes ‘nature.’

Bill McKibben

The photographs in this book were made in and around Secaucus, New Jersey between 2015 and 2020.

Thanks to Eugene and all of the friends who welcomed me over the years.

Special thanks to Matthew Casteel, Janet Delaney, Hartford Art School, Ward Long, Sam Margevicius, Accra Shepp, Victor Sira, Alec Soth, and Michael Vahrenwald

Published by
Hirmer Publishers
Bayerstrasse 57–59
80335 Munich
Germany
www.hirmerpublishers.com

Design Nicholas Pollack
Typesetting Hirmer Publishers
Copyediting and proof reading Jane Michael
Senior Editor at Hirmer Publishers Elisabeth Rochau-Shalem
Project Manager at Hirmer Publishers Rainer Arnold

Lithography and pre-press Reproline Mediateam, Unterföhring
Printing and binding Printer Trento s.r.l.
Paper GardaMatt Art 150 g/m²

Printed in Italy

ISBN 978-3-7774-3994-5